Praise for Bernard S. Brown's

Exploring Philly ~~Nature~~

"*Exploring Philly Nature* is a c   ...esources
of the Greater Philadelphia reg   ... nands-on
opportunities for exploration ar.   ...ner at home, in the
street, or in one of Philadelphia's .   ...ous metro-area parks and
preserves. Season by season, Brown guides the reader through the
whole tapestry of urban nature. Under his guidance, eagles, fireflies,
street rats, roadkill, and more provide an opportunity for people of all
ages to experience the joy of inquiry, adventure, and discovery."

—Maura McCarthy, PhD,
Executive Director of the Fairmount Park Conservancy

"No one knows Philly like Billy Brown. He has stuck his nose into
every corner of the city in search of wildlife and now has compiled
what he has learned and shared it here for the benefit of all. The result
is a masterful book that any novice or pro can use to begin exploring
Philadelphia in a whole new way, while still making discoveries of
their own. The tone of the book makes it accessible, approachable,
and useful for layperson and expert alike, whether you're searching
for bald eagles, scarce plants and wildflowers, butterflies, or even
slime molds. Brown draws on his years of experience and his
network of Philly naturalists to create a great guide to exploring and
understanding how Philly functions both as an ecosystem and a place
where still many discoveries remain to be made. Brown shows how
using nature as a filter for how we view Philadelphia changes how we
see it, making you cherish it all the more."

—George Armistead,
cofounder of BirdPhilly and author of the *American Birding
Association Field Guide to the Birds of Pennsylvania*

"*Exploring Philly Nature* is a portal to the everyday natural world found in every corner of Philadelphia. It is a wonderful guide to explore nature, from the cracks in our sidewalks to widely known places like the Wissahickon to lesser known natural gems in area neighborhoods. A marvelous resource for every nature enthusiast, it is a must for parents, guardians, teachers, and others to share the 'sense of wonder' of nature with kids. Brown includes a thoughtful 'kids' note in each profile as a guide to teach the young—and young at heart—that the joys of nature are all around us."

—Leigh Altadonna, EdD,
President of the Wyncote Audubon Society

Exploring Philly Nature

TEMPLE UNIVERSITY PRESS
Philadelphia • *Rome* • *Tokyo*

Exploring Philly Nature

A Guide for All Four Seasons

Bernard S. Brown

Illustrations by Samantha Wittchen

TEMPLE UNIVERSITY PRESS
Philadelphia, Pennsylvania 19122
tupress.temple.edu

Copyright © 2022 by Temple University—Of The Commonwealth System
   of Higher Education
All rights reserved
Published 2022

Text design by Samantha Wittchen

Library of Congress Cataloging-in-Publication Data

Names: Brown, Bernard S., 1976– author. | Wittchen, Samantha, illustrator.
Title: Exploring Philly nature : a guide for all four seasons / Bernard S.
   Brown ; illustrations by Samantha Wittchen.
Description: Philadelphia : Temple University Press, 2022. | Includes
   bibliographical references and index. | Summary: "Exploring Philly
   Nature is an amateur naturalist's guide to Greater Philadelphia, with a
   particular focus on getting families involved in exploring the urban
   natural world together"—Provided by publisher.
Identifiers: LCCN 2021040412 (print) | LCCN 2021040413 (ebook) |
   ISBN 9781439921210 (paperback) | ISBN 9781439921227 (pdf)
Subjects: LCSH: Natural history—Pennsylvania—Philadelphia—Guidebooks. |
   Nature study—Pennsylvania—Philadelphia. | Philadelphia
   (Pa.)—Description and travel. | LCGFT: Guidebooks.
Classification: LCC QH105.P4 B76 2022 (print) | LCC QH105.P4 (ebook) |
   DDC 508.748/11—dc23/eng/20211108
LC record available at https://lccn.loc.gov/2021040412
LC ebook record available at https://lccn.loc.gov/2021040413

♾ The paper used in this publication meets the requirements of the American National
Standard for Information Sciences—Permanence of Paper for Printed Library Materials,
ANSI Z39.48–1992

Printed in the United States of America

9 8 7 6 5 4 3 2 1

To Murray and Magnolia

Table of Contents

Exploring Philly Nature

Introduction

A Letter to the Reader

IF YOU'RE LIKE ME, you might have grown up watching nature documentaries. On the screen, you saw animals do amazing things in incredible places. Lions stalked zebras on the plains of East Africa. Perentie monitor lizards crept through the spinifex in the Australian Outback. Sloths hung from branches eighty feet up in the Amazon Basin. No rowhouses, skyscrapers, or concrete sidewalks made it into those documentaries, so you, like I, could be excused for assuming that nature was something "out there," not here in the middle of a major metropolitan area of more than six million people.

Luckily, we were wrong. I can't argue against the lure of the exotic places and the charismatic fauna in those documentaries, but the natural world offers us plenty to enjoy and learn from right here where we live.

Within a fifteen-minute bike ride of my house in West Philadelphia's Walnut Hill neighborhood, I can watch Cooper's hawks hunt pigeons, I can catch snakes, I can listen to warbling vireos sing as they hunt insects along a creek, I can paddle on a river while short-nosed sturgeon and American eels swim below, and I can pick wildflowers while migrating monarch and buckeye butterflies drink nectar around me.

It has taken me sixteen years to figure this out. When I first moved to Philadelphia, I sought my experiences with nature outside the city. I drove out to the Pine Barrens or the Poconos, where I enjoyed the vistas and looked for reptiles and amphibians ("herping"—thus, I am a "herper"). When I got home to my apartment, I stopped looking.

Over the years, I realized that there were snakes, salamanders, and turtles right here too. I started a blog about herping in Philadelphia, which led to writing about urban nature for *Grid*, a Philly environmental magazine. Researching articles for *Grid* introduced me to urban conservationists and environmental educators. I made friends with birders with impressive urban yard lists. I met plant lovers who taught me about what grew all around us in our parks as well as in our gardens and sidewalks. I bought an inflatable kayak that I could take down to the Delaware and the Schuylkill Rivers.

I have chosen to raise my children in a place rich with nature: a block in West Philadelphia lined with century-old twin houses. We listen to singing starlings and cardinals on the walk to school. We watch the butterflies and bees that visit the flowers in our garden and in the planters along the sidewalk. We admire the wildflowers in the vacant lot on the corner. For a week in the fall, we run upstairs right after dinner to a window with a perfect vantage point to see dozens of swifts pour into a chimney a block away. We talk about whether this will be the last night that they roost here on their way to South America. Of course, we also go hiking in conventional green spaces, but we never stop observing and learning from the natural world.

I hope that this book accelerates this process for you and your family. Maybe you are new to exploring nature in general or are looking to connect with the natural world closer to home. Maybe you are a birder or a gardener looking to expand your focus to other living things. Maybe you're looking for a way to connect your city kids to nature. Whatever brings you to this book, I hope that the activities in the following pages take you further on your journey to connecting with nature, wherever you are. You still might watch the newest BBC nature documentary. You, like I, will probably still take vacations to conventionally wild places and seek experiences with nature there. But when you get home, you'll keep on looking.

Urban Habitats

THE CONCRETE JUNGLE

Everywhere is habitat, and habitat is everywhere. While you will certainly have no trouble occupying your attention in official park spaces, where you will find the sorts of habitat types generally covered in nature books (wetlands, meadows, streams, upland forest, and so forth), you can also engage in the same nature observation activities without leaving your neighborhood—and in many cases, without even leaving your block.

Start with your home. In every human home, animals find a way to live, although they might be smaller than you would usually notice. If you have a basement, consider it to be a cave and explore it with a flashlight, searching for the spiders, crickets, and other arthropods adapted for darkness; cool, damp conditions; and little in the way of food. If you have no basement, take a look behind furniture and along windowsills for spiders spinning webs to catch unlucky flies, beetles, and moths.

Step outside onto the sidewalk. The brick and stone surfaces of your house or apartment building can host lichens, and the cracks in the sidewalk can sprout small plants. If you have trees, you will have squirrels, not to mention more lichens on the bark. Depending on the species (for example, lindens, redbuds, or ornamental cherries), their flowers will attract bees, butterflies, and other pollinators. You will also have birds: house sparrows, starlings, and pigeons to start with; chimney swifts in the summer; and larger species, such as crows, gulls, and birds of prey. In one hour in May, a friend and I spotted twelve species of bird at the end of my block in densely built West Philadelphia.

If you have a garden, you have plenty to explore. Spare your weeds as long as you can and figure out what they are. As plants flower, watch what flies in for the pollen and nectar. Any object that you can look underneath (stones, storage bins, straw bales, and so forth) will hide an assortment of invertebrates, such as centipedes, pill bugs, and beetles. You might even turn up a brown snake or a salamander. At night, possums, raccoons, and other nocturnal mammals might wander through to munch on those smaller critters (not to mention your tomatoes). You can string up a sheet for a moth night (see "What They Do in the Dark: Hold a Moth Night" for tips). Sit out in summer and watch the fireflies light up the dark. By day, dragonflies will zip along your block. A vacant lot can offer nearly as much to observe. Sparrows—native white-throated sparrows and juncos as well as house sparrows—might feed on weed and grass seeds through the winter. The flowering plants will grow and bloom in a shifting array of colors in the spring, at least until someone gets around to mowing.

Your local park, even if it's just grass with some tree cover, is worth birding. The same goes for cemeteries. Hawks will wait in the trees for unwary squirrels and pigeons. Spring and fall migration will bring dozens of species of songbirds on their journeys north and south. Watch dead branches high in the trees for woodpeckers. As night falls, bats might flap into view to feast on flying insects.

ABOVE AND BELOW THE FALL LINE

Anyone who has ridden a bicycle around Philadelphia has noticed the shift from coastal plain to piedmont. South Philadelphia, Southwest Philadelphia, Center City, and most of North Philadelphia are flat and easy to pedal across in one gear, and the same goes for the Northeast Philly neighborhoods close to the Delaware River. However, ride west on Spruce Street or Ridge Avenue, and you might need to downshift.

The falls of the Schuylkill, now Fairmount Dam, mark the "fall line," the boundary between the sandy, gravely ground of the coastal plain to the east and south and the rocky hills of the Wissahickon Formation (mostly schist and gneiss[1] under the soil) rising to the

---

1. U.S. Geological Survey, "Geological Units in Philadelphia County, Pennsylvania," accessed October 29, 2020, https://mrdata.usgs.gov/geology/state/fips-unit .php?code=f42101.

west and north. The fall line extends northeast to Trenton, New Jersey, and southwest to the Delaware state line.

The creeks and rivers of the piedmont tumble over small water*falls* as they transition to slower, coastal waterways—hence, "fall line." The force of falling water was once essential to powering industry. In 1645, nearly forty years before William Penn drafted the plans for Philadelphia, the Swedish governor Johann Printz built a mill on Cobbs Creek (then known only by the Lenape name "Karakung") where today Woodland Avenue crosses from Philadelphia into Delaware County. European settlers continued to build mills at and upstream from the fall line, and the remains of that early industrial infrastructure are still visible today as you hike along our creeks. For example, as you walk the Orange Trail in the Wissahickon past Glen Fern, you'll notice where the creek pools behind an old dam. There, you can see the ruins of Thomas Livezy's eighteenth-century mill. The creek banks, less obviously human-made than the stone ruins of the mills and dams, are nonetheless artifacts of this early industrial past. The low stone dams constructed along these creeks to impound mill ponds filled in with silt over the centuries, building up the valley bottoms. As most of the dams have broken down, the creeks have cut their courses down through accumulated sediments.[2] Thus, our creek corridor parks, enjoyed as natural spaces, are themselves thoroughly postindustrial landscapes.

THE WATER

You might eventually get on or in the water, but the easiest way to check out a creek or river is to stop on a bridge the next time you get a chance and take a look around. This might be the closest you can get to the water without getting in. The Schuylkill and the

---

2. Robert C. Walter and Dorothy J. Merritts, "Natural Streams and the Legacy of Water-Powered Mills," *Science* 319, no. 5861 (January 18, 2008): 299–304, doi:10.1126/science.1151716.

Delaware Rivers are also accessible (in the sense that you can get close to the water's edge) from multiuse trails and old piers, such as Pier 53 in South Philadelphia. Examine logs or old timbers that stick out of the water for basking turtles in warm, sunny weather. Canals, built to transport goods in the years before railroads, are often maintained today as accessible aquatic habitats, with multiuse trails along the Schuylkill and Delaware Rivers above the fall line.

Note the birds that float on, swim in, or fly just over the water. In the summer, swallows will swoop and zip, picking insects out of the air. Waterfowl (such as ducks and geese) will rest or swim on the surface, particularly in the winter, when birds from the north head south, looking for unfrozen water. Cormorants, black birds with long, snakelike necks and yellow bills like spears, will dive and catch fish underwater.

Our murky waterways are generally inaccessible from above, but our creeks, particularly in their shallows, are clear enough to observe the fish swimming in them. From above, you can spot the swimming shapes of various sizes, and in spring and summer, you might even spot a red-breasted sunfish guarding its nest of carefully cleared stream bottom. Frogs and toads will sing from the edge of the water, particularly bullfrogs and green frogs by summer. You can often spot their large tadpoles in the shallows. Watch the dragonflies and damselflies as well. As I write this, forty-seven species of these colorful hunters have been logged on iNaturalist in Philadelphia.

Fishing, of course, is one way to explore the diversity swimming below wherever you are, but also keep an eye out for piles of mussel shells and clamshells left by raccoons and otters. And take a look before you brush off the flying insects that land on you. The caddisflies, mayflies, stoneflies, midges, and others are brief adult phases of critters that spend most of their lives beneath the water, and they themselves feed everything from bridge spiders to the swallows that catch them out of the air and the yellow warblers that pick them off the trees lining the shore.

Paddling a canoe or a kayak on our rivers puts you at the water's surface. This can be a great vantage point to observe aquatic waterlife, such as basking turtles and waterfowl. Fish jump right in front of you, and bugs and birds (such as tree swallows) fly at eye level. Inexperienced paddlers should start with guided trips as they get the hang of maneuvering a boat on rivers with big currents. Also, keep an eye on water quality. Storms flush all sorts of pollutants into the river, and for a few days after a heavy rain, you'll want to avoid contact with the water. Check PhillyRiverCast.org, a water-quality forecast tool, before you put in.

FOREST

Neglect any piece of ground long enough in our area, and it will probably end up as forest. Of course, the forest will vary, depending on where you are. Along our creeks and rivers, you might find willows, eastern cottonwoods, and such exotics as princess trees and mulberries. In hillier landscapes, oak, beech, and tulip trees might dominate the canopy. You can find some hemlocks in the Wissahickon Valley, along with stands of white pines. Virtually all of these forests are young, growing on land cleared for farming and industry as Europeans colonized the Delaware Valley. For example, the Wissahickon Valley, which today can feel like the forest primeval with towering oak and tulip trees, was protected as parkland starting in the mid-1800s, and those stately white pine trees were likely planted intentionally, not having been found in the area previously.[3]

Whatever their species composition, our forests offer so much to explore. The trees themselves can be hugged and admired. Ephemeral wildflowers color the forest floor before those trees leaf out in the spring and block out the sun. In the autumn, wood asters and white snakeroots brighten up the browns and oranges of falling leaves. The leaf litter and the rotting logs of the forest floor fuel their own hidden ecosystem, with a wide variety of invertebrates

---

3. David Hewitt, "The White Pines of Cresheim Creek," *Growing History*, June 22, 2012, accessed October 29, 2020, https://growinghistory.wordpress.com/2012/06/22/the-white-pines-of-cresheim-creek/.

and inconspicuous vertebrates, such as red-backed salamanders and American toads. Lichens grow on the tree bark, and mushrooms sprout from dead wood and the forest floor. You can spot our larger mammals, such as the overly abundant white-tailed deer, and, of course, there are plenty of birds to watch and listen to.

MEADOW

A visitor from Independence-era Philadelphia might be shocked at the scarcity of meadows (let's pretend that they wouldn't be fixated on automobiles, skyscrapers, and people baring their legs). Back when Philadelphia was mostly farmland, pastures and hayfields served as economically active land as well as habitats for plants and animals that are now scarce in our area. Today, vacant land often sprouts relatively sterile monocultures of mugwort or gets swamped by other exotic plants, such as Japanese hops. All this makes our existing meadows, generally actively managed to maintain a mix of native grasses and forbs (leafy plants), all the more special. You can listen to field sparrows trill in the spring. Through the summer, milkweed patches attract hordes of pollinators and host gorgeous monarch butterflies. In the fall, you can see the goldenrod and other fall wildflowers paint the fields in bright yellow. By winter, all the seeds of these flowers and grasses will feed native sparrows, including white-throated sparrows and juncos. You can also find patches of meadow in other infrequently mowed spots, such as along power line rights-of-way.

WETLAND

Below the fall line, Philadelphia used to be a lot wetter than it is now. Much of South Philadelphia, including the Philadelphia International Airport, has been built on wetlands drained or filled in to create solid land. Our tidal waterways are now largely defined by "bulwarked" infrastructure. The shores rise steeply in concrete and timber walls or have been reinforced by riprap—rocks or the brick and concrete remains of demolished buildings, dumped to stabilize the banks. You can still explore wetlands at the John Heinz National Wildlife Refuge at Tinicum, which straddles Philadelphia and Delaware County. Smaller patches of marsh are accessible at other sites, such as Fort Mifflin and Cramer Hill Preserve in Camden, and in between piers along the Delaware River waterfront, where the still water allows sediment to settle out and marsh vegetation to take root.

The challenge of wetlands is that they are difficult to walk through, so you need to observe them either from neighboring land or water. For example, the John Heinz National Wildlife Refuge at Tinicum offers boardwalks and trails along levees to get you as close by foot as possible without sinking into the muck. Paddling offers a closeup look at marshy shorelines, whether you're in the back channel of the Delaware River in New Jersey or in the mouth of the Pennypack on the other side.

Urban Life and How to Observe It

You can start by simply looking around and listening. While there are many techniques to observing the natural world, staying still and quiet while you use your senses is easy, free, and useful. As your ears and eyes adjust to the setting, details emerge that you otherwise would have missed.

I am frequently amazed at how close animals will get to me when I stop moving. This is usually unintentional on my part because I have trouble sitting still. I'll stop for a drink of water and check my phone, or I'll freeze in place as I try to locate a warbler that just sang high up in a tree. Then, I'll hear something rustling in the underbrush, and out pops a squirrel. Browsing deer will gradually work their way in my direction until I flinch. Then, with a snort, they bound away.

All that being said, trying out specialized observation techniques can reveal more about the natural world, whether you are in your garden or in the middle of a forest. For more detail, check out specific guidebooks, but this overview and the examples in the suggested activities can get you started.

In general, take care with methods that involve disturbing the organism that you are observing. We have regulations on fishing (seasons, catch limits, and so forth) so that populations aren't affected and enough remains for other people to enjoy. Similarly, our parks often limit what you can pick, catch, or take home due to the high volume of visitors and their potential impact. When in doubt, consult with specialists to see what level of disturbance is too much in particular settings.

PLANTS, FUNGI, LICHENS, AND SLIME MOLDS

In many ways, it is easiest to observe things that don't move. Plants, fungi, lichens, and even slime molds stay still while you look at them. There's no need to sneak up on them, and you can take your time examining them.

In urban landscapes, it helps to think small. On sidewalks, plants survive the constant trampling by growing in cracks and keeping a low profile. Often, you can find plants growing and flowering as tiny versions of what you'll find elsewhere. Not surprisingly, our solid surfaces of brick, concrete, and stone grow more hospitable as they age, so pay extra attention to old stone walls for mosses, lichens, and ferns and inspect older sidewalks for plants growing from the cracks. The same can be true of street surfaces. Old brick, cobblestone, or Belgian block road surfaces, which often survive in alleys or driveways, host a jungle of tiny plants in the sandy gaps between the individual pieces.

You might feel overwhelmed as you look at all the plants growing in a green field, vacant lot, forest understory, or even a weedy garden. One technique that botanists use is to intensively search a smaller plot—say, a square meter in area—and catalogue everything growing in it. You don't have to be quite so rigorous, but narrowing your focus to a manageable scale can help you get past the showier plants that catch your eye and pay attention to smaller or plainer species. Similar approaches can work just off the ground as you search for lichens, fungi, and slime molds. You might study the lichens growing on one tree's trunk, or you might spend some focused time searching for mushrooms and slime molds on one rotting log, carefully checking all its surfaces and peering under loose bark.

While you might have no trouble finding trees, you might miss a lot of the action if you only glance at the trunks as you walk by. Low twigs can offer a look at the development of leaves, flowers, and then fruit. We tend to ignore tree flowers that are up high, out of sight, but insects do not. The flowers of many of our trees, such as willows, offer pollen and nectar to bees early in the spring. Others, such as cherries and black locusts, might have showy blossoms that humans like to look at, but you might miss the orange flowers of the tulip tree mixed in with the leaves high in the canopy. Be sure to look for them.

Vining plants, often considered nuisances when they're growing on your house or fence, are similarly important and easy to ignore. Cities are full of vertical surfaces that trumpet flower, porcelain berry, and honeysuckle can climb. Virginia creeper's inconspicuous flowers offer nectar to pollinators, and their dark blue berries feed birds from fall into the winter.

Of course, immobility is not the same as permanence, and much of the fun of exploring nature is seeing how landscapes and organisms change through the seasons. A vacant lot will reward your attention with a shifting palette of flowers: pink dead nettles at the end of winter, then white flowers of shepherd's purse reaching higher as a haze above the ground, later to be topped by yellow dandelion and white and lavender fleabanes. You can also track individual plants or patches of plants through the year. The Virginia jumpseed that starts out as a few glossy leaves sprouting out of the forest floor sports a whiplike spike of small white flowers in the middle of the summer. In the fall, those flowers end up as little football-shaped seeds that shoot out like bullets when touched.

Fungi and slime molds are difficult to observe most of the time. The mushrooms or visually striking slime-mold features that catch our attention are the spore-producing structures of creatures that carry out the rest of their business out of sight. Fungi are primarily networks of threadlike structures called hyphae that spread in soil or wood. Slime molds might be spread out and inconspicuous as they ooze around and consume single-celled organisms and decaying matter. Thus, you might walk past the same rotting stump for most of the year and only notice the bright orange chicken of the woods growing out of it on a damp day in early fall. You might then take a closer look at a chocolate tube slime mold that likewise just became visible to you, while both organisms have spent all year feeding on or in the stump. In general, dry weather is bad for fungi and slime molds. A good soaking after a dry spell can bring forth a bloom of mushrooms.

You generally won't need binoculars, but magnification can still help. There is always more detail to be revealed at a smaller scale. Even on our largest trees, tiny buds and leaf scars can be the key to identification. The small parts of flowers can vary importantly, and what looks like a simple patch of gray lichen can be seen reproducing through cuplike structures if you look closely enough. Handheld magnifying glasses or loupes can do the trick, but these days, so can the zoom feature on a smartphone camera.

Be sure to look at the whole organism, even underneath. Common blue violets, for example, might dazzle with their namesake blooms, but they also hide plain, pale flowers close to the soil. Mushroom identification often depends on what's underneath: gills or pores? Some species of goldenrod can be differentiated by the fuzziness of their stems, and the same can be true of the shape of the little scalelike bracts under an aster.

Multiple apps, some powered by artificial intelligence, can help you make an identification simply by uploading a photograph. Working out the identification on your own, however, will help you learn the key differences between species and teach you something about their natural history in the process. If you can't take the organism home, then take lots of pictures or notes, taking care to observe all its parts. It can be frustrating to get home and realize that you forgot to check some key feature, such as whether the leaves were attached with petioles (little stalks at their base), so err on the side of thoroughness.

Studying a plant from an established path is a low-impact activity for the plants and their habitat. Be careful as you tromp off into the woods or meadows, though, because heavy traffic can disturb leaf litter, erode the forest floor, and even damage plants that you might be looking for. Follow rules for official park spaces and use your judgment about how popular a spot is. If you're the only person who walks through that patch of woods all year, you probably aren't causing much damage, but the more people do it, the more damage they cause. Similar judgment should apply to picking plant or mushroom specimens to examine at home. Yanking a goldenrod from a vacant lot or power line right-of-way doesn't make much of a difference, but if everyone visiting Houston Meadow came home with a bouquet, it might actually degrade the view and experience for other visitors. Again, follow rules for official park spaces and, when in doubt, explore with guided groups and ask the leader for their more expert opinion on what you can and should pick.

The Philly area is blessed with active clubs devoted to plants (the Philadelphia Botanical Club) and fungi (the Philadelphia Mycology Club). Both offer a full schedule of walks and events, as do our local arboretums, parks, and nature centers.

FISH AND OTHER AQUATIC ORGANISMS

Aquatic habitats are the most difficult to observe. We generally cannot explore under the water without breathing aids, such as snorkels, and the water is often too green or brown to see through.

When and where we can see into the water—for example, from bridges over shallow water—we can watch fish swimming, feeding, breeding, and generally carrying on their lives. Polarized sunglasses can help cut the glare coming off the water. The Fairmount Dam Fishway camera, when it is operational in the spring, films fish and other animals swimming up the Fishway (a rising series of compartments that allows shad to make it over the dam and swim upstream) and gives us a peek under the water.

We are often limited to what we can bring to the surface—most commonly, fish—making fishing a valuable way to learn about what is down there. Ichthyologists will use particularly thorough methods, such as electrofishing (running a current through the water that stuns all the fish in the vicinity). Multispecies fishing, which is the approach of trying to catch as many species of fish as possible in a particular body of water, can help you learn a little more about the fish actually below the surface. By varying bait and tackle (including using "microfishing" tackle for smaller fish species), you can get beyond the usual channel catfish and smallmouth bass. Under a multispecies fishing approach, any body of water is worth fishing, whether that's a lake surrounded by forested hills or a creek surrounded by rowhouses. Consider bringing along a small aquarium or large jar to place catches into. That way, you can observe them for a moment before releasing them. A fish in its element is much more beautiful than one flopping at the end of a line. Leo Sheng, known as "Extreme Philly Fishing" on social media, is a proponent of multispecies fishing, and his videos and blog posts are an excellent introduction.

Guided fishing events offer a way to get started without gear or a license, but be sure to get a fishing license and learn about species-specific seasons and catch limits once you decide to strike out on your own. Luckily, the agencies that regulate fishing are eager to get more people into the hobby and welcome beginners looking to learn more about how to fish safely and legally.

SMALL LAND INVERTEBRATES

Insects, spiders, and other invertebrates are stupendously diverse, and so are the methods scientists have devised to capture and observe them. I'll touch on a few here.

Diurnal pollinators, such as butterflies and bees, make it easy. Park yourself next to some flowers and see who flies in. In spring, be sure to pay attention to flowering trees. In summer, milkweed patches can be particularly productive, and don't give up in the fall. Late-flowering asters, for example, bring in bees and butterflies into November.

Look under surface objects. When you're small and vulnerable to predators and the drying heat of the sun, you tend to hide during the day. Thus, lifting a flowerpot in a garden or a board in a vacant lot can reveal a small menagerie of crickets, spiders, centipedes, mollusks (snails and slugs), and beetles. The same can be true of checking the undersides of plants, where lots of critters hide during the day or when they're otherwise resting.

It might feel strange to use binoculars to look at something ten feet away, but they can come in handy to watch butterflies without spooking them. The same is true of the dragonflies and damselflies you can observe around water.

Consider investing $20 or so in an insect net. You can use these to catch such insects as butterflies or dragonflies in the air for a closer look, and you can also sweep vegetation and take a closer look at what you catch in a jar.

Take advantage of inadvertent bug traps. Insects fall into fountains and swimming pools, but they rarely get out alive. This is, of course, sad for them, but it means that a small aquarium net is all you need to take a closer look at the drowned critters. Indeed, entomologist Isa Betancourt undertook a multiyear study of the bugs that drowned in the Swann Fountain in Logan Circle in Philadelphia.[4]

The nighttime is the right time to observe moths and lots of other nocturnal critters. You can do this with the sheet-and-light setup described in the Moth Night section, but also be sure to use your ears. With a little practice, you can distinguish the various crickets, katydids, and cicadas that we too often let slip into the background of our evening soundtracks but are singing all around us, particularly in the summer.

---

4. Isa Betancourt, "The Philadelphia Fountain Insect Survey," The Bug and the Beetle, accessed October 29, 2020, http://www.thebugandthebeetle.net/research.

The Academy of Natural Sciences of Drexel University offers arthropod programming through the year, including at Bug Fest events at its museum as well as social media content to help the backyard butterfly watcher.

REPTILES AND AMPHIBIANS

Quiet watching works well for some reptiles and amphibians, particularly for species active during the day, such as garter snakes, and those that bask in the open, such as larger turtles.

Listening is an important way to observe frogs and toads, particularly during the spring and summer. Wood frogs and spring peepers kick off the action as the ground begins to thaw, and bullfrogs and green frogs call well into the summer. Although many will call in the daytime, evenings are best, and so is wet weather. Calling amphibians will often shut up when they hear or see you. Luckily, they will stop noticing you if you stop moving. Freeze for a couple of minutes, and they'll pick up their singing again.

Herpers (people who recreationally seek out reptiles and amphibians, known as "herping") spend a lot of time looking under surface objects for critters hiding underneath, "flipping," as in "flipping rocks" or "flipping boards." Indeed, whatever the habitat, it's worth looking under stuff. If you're in the garden, you could turn up a brown snake. In a meadow, you might find garter snakes and milk snakes. In forests, you'll find woodland salamanders, toads, and ringneck snakes. Near aquatic habitats, you can find a variety of amphibians as well as water snakes.

Whatever the habitat, follow a few rules to avoid injuring the critters you find or ruining their habitat:

- Always reposition what you flip exactly the way you found it.
- Always move critters out of the way before you replace a heavy object so that you don't squash them. They will find their way back underneath on their own.
- Related to the previous rule, be careful to avoid lifting objects

too heavy to hold up with one hand while you manipulate the animals with the other.

If you plan to capture and examine a reptile or amphibian, it can help to have a clear container to put it into for the closer look. A garter snake biting and pooping all over you calms down pretty quickly in a jar, and you can then take your photos or pass it to other people before you release it. Amphibians in particular can have extremely delicate skin. A clean jar protects them from us. Be sure to clean jars when you get home with a little bleach and water and let them dry thoroughly before the next use. Also, be sure to punch holes in the jar lids from the inside, so that any sharp edges project out and don't cut the captured critters.

Remember to consult state regulations on catching reptiles and amphibians if you decide to focus on herping. In Pennsylvania, for example, catching any reptile or amphibian requires a fishing license. Luckily, fishing licenses are inexpensive and support much of the state's reptile and amphibian conservation work.

Unfortunately, many species are vulnerable to poaching. Park rangers or game officers can't always distinguish between someone catching a snake to take some photos and a poacher catching it to sell. Rules often restrict catching them at all, regardless of the reason. Whatever the state-level regulations, when you're in a park setting, observe the rules of the park.

Some snakes and turtles can be dangerous. It takes some care to handle a large snapping turtle, and smaller species, such as stinkpots, will clamp down on your hand if you let them. More challenging are venomous snakes. Luckily for the beginning herper, venomous snakes only reach the fringes of the Philadelphia suburbs: copperheads in Pennsylvania and timber rattlers in the Pine Barrens of New Jersey, both beyond the reach of this guidebook. When in doubt, don't pick it up, and remember that any snake you see is no threat to you. You can always move around it.

Of course, starting with guided walks led by experts is a great way to learn the rules wherever you are and to handle critters safely.

At the time of writing, the Pennsylvania Amphibian and Reptile Survey (PARS), run by the Mid-Atlantic Center for Herpetology and Conservation (MACHAC) in partnership with the Pennsylvania Fish and Boat Commission, collects observations of reptiles and amphibians to help guide research and conservation efforts. You can contribute your observations directly at https://paherpsurvey.org or by joining the PARS project in iNaturalist.

BIRDS

Start by listening and watching around your block, as described in the "Rats with Wings and Other Common Birds: Start Birding Anytime" entry. Birds are around us wherever we are, and you can get a lot of practice observing them from the sidewalk outside your home. Pretty soon, you'll notice other, less abundant birds, whether migrants passing through or seasonal residents, such as chimney swifts in the summer or white-throated sparrows in the winter.

Use your ears as much as your eyes. Sometimes, this is the only way to distinguish visually similar species. Philadelphia is full of American crows and fish crows, but I had no idea which was which until I learned to pick out the more nasal calls of the fish crows. Many birds announce their presence and their ownership of a territory. For example, the iconic, high-pitched scream of a red-tailed hawk will let you know to look up and find it wheeling overhead. Many birds sing during their breeding season or while they're migrating north, and those songs are often the only clue you have that they're around. You can easily hear the lovely song of the warbling vireo near the water at parks throughout our region, but it takes a lot more effort and patience to actually spot them hunting for bugs in the trees.

Binoculars are incredibly helpful in birding. You can check binoculars out of many Free Library of Philadelphia branches for use at home, and nature centers and other groups that sponsor birding walks often provide a few extra pairs for beginners. Keep in mind that you tend to initially find birds with the ear or the naked eye. Once you hear one or see it moving, lift the binoculars to take a closer look.

Myriad guidebooks and apps help you identify birds that you find. Whatever you use, consider documenting your finds in citizen science apps, such as iNaturalist or eBird, or by participating in such events as a Christmas Bird Count (or Philadelphia's Winter Bird Census). Your observation, even one from the sidewalk on your block, could end up as a useful data point for research or conservation efforts.

Birders tend to flock together, for better or for worse. Social media helps spread news of rare visitors or hotspots during migration, and before you know it, a small crowd forms, bristling with spotting scopes and high-powered zoom lenses. This can be helpful for the beginner, as such popular spots as the John Heinz National Wildlife Refuge at Tinicum will usually have someone around who can tell you about what they are watching.

Once you get the hang of observing birds, though, please consider branching out to less birded spots. Our region is full of green spaces whose biodiversity hasn't been well documented, and you can help fill in these blank spots on the map by simply birding close to where you already are. Most importantly, never give up simply because you don't have the time to travel to a conventional hotspot. I got started birding at the Independence National Historical Park in Old City because it was close to my office, and I could pop out during my lunch breaks. I now frequently bird at Malcolm X Park in West Philadelphia, simply because it is near my house. Neither of these parks looks particularly wild (mostly grass, trees, and ornamental shrubs), but I usually find more than enough birds to keep me happily occupied.

Thanks to the popularity of birding, more birding resources are available than for nearly any other corner of the natural world. The Delaware Valley Ornithological Club (DVOC) offers meetings and guided walks year-round. The DVOC partners with Philadelphia Parks and Recreation to lead the BirdPhilly walk series at Philly parks. New birding groups, including the In Color Birding Club, Philly Queer Birders, Adapted Birding, and a local chapter of the Feminist Bird Club, are welcoming an expanded community of birders. Nature centers and parks offer birding programming as well. Outside the city, check your local Audubon chapter for its own schedule of walks and events.

MAMMALS

I'll bet that the wild urban creatures you know best are mammals. These could be the mice and rats you wish didn't live with you, but more likely, these are the squirrels you see every day, year-round. Most wild urban mammals (I'm excluding pet species and, of course, humans) follow rule number one of urban animal survival: Stay out of sight. Squirrels don't. They carry out most of their lives in plain view. You can watch them gather acorns (or raid your trash), you can watch them play, and you can watch them get eaten by hawks. Their nests in tree cavities can be hard to find, but others you can spot as big wads of leaves up in trees, particularly in fall and winter.

Going beyond watching squirrels can take a little more effort and patience. Most of our other mammal neighbors are active when we generally are not. A walk around your neighborhood at night (or just at dawn, if that is safer) can turn up rabbits, raccoons, skunks, opossums, coyotes, and foxes that stay out of sight during the day.

Likewise, visiting your nearest park at dawn or dusk can be productive. Deer are more likely to be out feeding, as are woodchucks. When you can, choose parks connected to other green spaces, whether by waterways or by railroads. These connections serve as corridors that expand habitat for animal populations.

During the day, learn about the local mammals by paying attention to their signs (clues they leave behind). Check sidewalks for animal prints left behind as the concrete set. Also, take a look at muddy patches in parks for prints of deer, raccoons, and other mammals mixed in with the prints of dogs and humans. In winter, get outside as soon as the snow stops to look for prints. Get to know your local animal scat (poop) as well. Deer leave plenty behind as they travel, and some animals, including foxes, defecate in prominent spots to mark their territory. What looks like dog poop but has fur in it can be a sign of local foxes and coyotes—dogs tend not to eat small animals whole.

A NOTE ON HUNTING

You might think of hunting as something people do out in the country, but hunting on private land is often legal in other landscapes. Urban hunters are generally folks who learned to hunt in the countryside but realized they could bag deer and turkeys here too.

I consider hunting to be a bit advanced for a guide targeted toward the beginning or casual naturalist, but if you'd like to get started, check with your state game agency. Some local parks, such as Ridley Creek State Park, do allow hunting, and the John Heinz National Wildlife Refuge at Tinicum has offered a bowhunting program for beginners.

Nature Activities

No matter what I include, this section is incomplete. Fifty-two activities fit well with the fifty-two weeks of the year, and they fit well in a relatively compact book.

In reality, though, there is no end to the ways you can connect to nature, even in a city. You can stake out your backyard for nocturnal mammals, but you can also bait tree trunks with peanut butter for flying squirrels or observe coyotes in wide open spaces, such as at Valley Forge. You can study lichens in a cemetery, but you could also follow the life cycle of mosses in sidewalk cracks. Please consider this book to be a sampling of ways to engage with nature rather than a comprehensive list.

Moreover, while urban habitats are distinctive, the techniques useful in a city are just as useful outside in more classically "wild" spaces. Keying out plants is the same wherever they grow. You can find brown snakes by flipping surface objects in gardens and vacant lots. In the Pine Barrens, you can find worm snakes the same way, just as you flip rocks for pale milk snakes in Montana.

With that in mind, many of these activities are easy to do at or near your home, outside official park spaces. For others, I recommend a place to take part in the activity, but these site recommendations are by no means exclusive. Riverfront North runs an introductory fishing program, but if you don't live near Northeast Philadelphia, you can do something similar at the John Heinz National Wildlife Refuge at Tinicum and Bartram's Garden, to name just a few possibilities. And, of course, you can easily get a fishing license and take your own gear to a body of water near you.

Most of these activities require little in the way of specialized equipment, and much of that, you can borrow. For example, if you want to go fishing, you'll need a rod and tackle, but the fishing programs I mention provide that for participants. Generally speaking, the most useful equipment to have is magnifying glasses and binoculars. Magnifying glasses are easy to find for under $10, but you can also use the camera on your smartphone or tablet to zoom in for magnification. Binoculars can be a bit more expensive, but you can check them out of several library branches, and many nature centers offer them for visitors to borrow.

You might notice that this book is a bit birding-heavy. There's a good reason: Habitat in cities is sliced into relatively small patches by our road networks, which, to earthbound creatures, are often insurmountable barriers. For example, much of Philadelphia and all of its suburbs would be perfect black rat snake habitat—plenty of trees and structures to climb, plenty of holes in buildings for hiding, and an endless supply of small, warm-blooded prey. But a slow, five-foot-long snake has little chance of successfully crossing a four-lane arterial road. Thus, in Philadelphia, we find black rat snakes at the fringes, close to strips of green space with little car traffic. Creatures that can disperse by air (including many insects as well as spiders that "balloon" as hatchlings) have an easier time crossing roads. Birds are also relatively large and conduct their business in the open, so birding offers the urban naturalist a lot of biodiversity to experience and enjoy.

Most of these activities are also suitable for children. Some might lend themselves better to older children rather than younger:

Flipping rocks and seeing what lives underneath is fun at any age, but patiently waiting in freezing weather for ducks to swim into view might take a little more maturity and a longer attention span. Nocturnal activities in particular might keep kids up past their bedtimes. I've added a note to each section about how kids might engage with the activity, but, of course, you know your kids better than I do. Use your own judgment about what makes sense for them.

Some of the programming I refer to might not be available when you read this. Organizations (nature centers, friends groups, clubs, and so forth) change over time, and so do their staffing, funding, opportunities, and priorities. Natural phenomena themselves are dynamic, so a meadow can become overgrown with trees, or a tree holding an eagle nest can blow down in a storm, forcing its inhabitants to move. Writing this book during the COVID-19 pandemic added an additional layer of uncertainty, with so much in-person programming suspended or modified. A particular walk series or annual event might end or be adapted to new circumstances, but I hope a little searching or asking around will turn up similar programming somewhere else.

I have organized these activity suggestions as follows:

- After an introduction, I provide an overview of the activity.
- I then cover the basic information you need to know before you get started (where, when, access considerations, needed equipment, how you can take part in a guided version of the activity, and resources to learn more).
- I note other locations in the area where you can take part.
- I end with a note on considerations for taking part with children.

I have tried to spread the site recommendations around geographically. Some of our larger parks, such as the Wissahickon Valley or the John Heinz National Wildlife Refuge at Tinicum, could, practically speaking, host almost all of these activities, but I hope you can find some examples near you wherever you are.

I. Winter

1

Go Birds!
Watch Bald Eagles Nesting

BIRDERS SOMETIMES COMPLAIN about all the nonbirders who excitedly tell them about seeing bald eagles. Bald eagles are actually pretty common and easy to find these days, but those who came of age in the 1980s or earlier, when then-scarce bald eagles were the poster children for the impact of the pesticide DDT, get particularly excited to see them. Count me among the excited. Our national symbol is a truly magnificent bird, with a huge wingspan and the most impressive weaponry Philly area naturalists will see on any animal: a massive, sharp beak and talons like curved daggers. I stop and gaze in amazement, even if I just saw one the day before.

A pair of bald eagles has claimed a huge sycamore tree on the edge of the restored wetland at the mouth of the Pennypack Creek (known as "Pennypack on the Delaware" [POD]). It's a logical place for a fish-eating eagle to nest, with both the creek and the mighty Delaware full of prey. It's also a great place to observe the eagles, with a multiuse path curving right past the other side of that restored wetland.

Although we might think of birds building nests and raising young in the spring, bald eagles get started much earlier in the winter. So, as soon as their namesake Eagles of football have been eliminated from playoff contention (again), spend a Sunday afternoon watching our wild eagles at work.

WHERE: POD is off State Road in Northeast Philadelphia. Once you park, walk north along the river past the playing fields and through the gate to the natural area. The viewing spot for the eagles' nest is at the edge of the wetlands, about six hundred yards past the gate.

ACCESS: The park is generally open during daylight hours and can be reached by car, SEPTA bus, or regional rail (Holmesburg Junction Station). The path back to where you can view the eagles is paved.

WHEN: Although the enormous nests that bald eagles build are visible year-round, the eagles lay eggs and raise nestlings from winter into early spring.

FOR MORE INFORMATION: Get in touch with Riverfront North (riverfrontnorth.org), an organization that develops green space and offers programming along the Delaware River waterfront in Northeast Philadelphia, to learn more about POD and its schedule of nature walks.

EQUIPMENT: Binoculars will come in handy but aren't essential. The multiuse path is flat and well maintained, so comfortable walking shoes will suffice.

GUIDED VIEWING: Riverfront North and other organizations offer guided nature walks at POD that include the eagles' nest. Contact Riverfront North to learn more about upcoming walks.

OTHER LOCATIONS: Bald eagles also commonly nest at the John Heinz National Wildlife Refuge at Tinicum, not to mention in Camden, New Jersey, at Farnham Park; on Petty's Island Preserve in the Delaware River; and at many other spots around the region. Wherever you watch them, be sure to keep a respectful distance. Bald eagles can get spooked by too many people close to their nests.

KIDS: A bald eagle is relatively easy to observe and get excited about. Everything about them is big: their bodies, their wings, their dramatic talons, and their nests.

2

Catch Creepy Crawlies
Hunt for Basement Bugs

WE TOOK A BREAK from a City Nature Challenge Organizing Committee meeting we were having in the dining room and headed down to the basement. I handed out flashlights. There are a lot of ways you might get up and stretch your legs when you've been sitting around a table talking for too long, and this particular evening, when it was dark and cold outside, we embarked on a basement critter hunt.

"Found a spider," someone called, peering behind some dusty object leaning against the wall. "Got a centipede," someone else offered. And so it went for five minutes, until it was time to get back to work. I collected the flashlights, and we headed back upstairs.

Habitat is all around us, even in our homes. The crumbs we drop, the mold that grows in damp corners, even the dead skin cells we shed fuel an ecosystem of small critters that we can observe without even getting dressed or putting on shoes. Basements, where we rarely tread and where undisturbed shelves and boxes provide a stable landscape, are fertile ground to explore this animal community. Bring a flashlight and magnifying glass and start looking. If you don't have a basement, try peeking behind furniture and appliances in quieter corners of your home.

A reliable, cosmopolitan group of species awaits, most of them originating in caves. Over the centuries, they have hitchhiked to destinations around the globe, ultimately settling in the artificial caves we build under our dwellings.

Cobweb spiders, such as the triangulate cobweb spider, hang out in tight spaces under furniture. Long-legged cellar spiders, looking a bit like daddy longlegs, drape the messy webs that your face catches as you rummage around for camping gear or holiday lights. House centipedes scurry away from the light like a cross between a race car and a dust bunny. All are there for you to study as they eat, reproduce, and otherwise carry on their lives.

WHERE: Your home

WHEN: Thanks to the stable temperatures year-round, you can find household spiders and other critters any time you want.

EQUIPMENT: A jar will help you capture and then observe delicate critters without the risk of crushing them with your hands. A flashlight will help, as will a magnifying glass to get a closer look. Wear whatever you want.

KIDS: So many young children start off interested in bugs and spiders, only to turn squeamish as they grow older. Nip that process in the bud by accompanying your kids on basement outings to learn about the utterly harmless spiders. Jars make it easy to catch a critter for a moment without harming it and protect fingers from the vanishingly small risk of a spider bite (black widows tend to spin webs in outside sheltered spaces, such as garages or tool sheds, rather than basements, and brown recluses are entirely absent from Philadelphia).

3

Step into the Shadows
Watch Rats

MORE THAN ONCE, I have seen something scurry through the shadows out of the corner of my eye as I've walked home from a bar. I have stood on a trolley or El platform at 30th Street Station and seen particularly bold rats working under the fluorescent lights to pick up the bits of food commuters drop onto the tracks. These are staple urban wildlife experiences, even if most urbanites recoil with horror and disgust at the sight of one of the most abundant spontaneously occurring mammals in our city.

Rats, like pigeons and house sparrows, are a prominent link in the urban food chain. They take nutrients that we throw away and, in turn, pass them along to hawks, foxes, coyotes, and other predators. When you watch the red-tailed hawks of the Benjamin Franklin Parkway, you are watching feathers and flesh built from digested rat meat, itself composed of pretzel crumbs, chicken wing scraps, and ice cream drips retrieved at night from the sidewalks.

Rats spend most of their lives in the dark, whether in our sewers, eating what we flush down the drains, or emerging above ground to raid our trash cans and dumpsters after dark. If you would like to observe them, stay up late or get up at dawn to see the rats make their final feeding runs.

No one advertises their rats (and, indeed, it is good public policy to reduce rat populations), but you can find them where we leave food out in the open. That might be human food, such as in dumpsters in the alleys behind restaurants or around trash cans in popular parks once the people have mostly gone home. It also can be animal food; feral cat feeding stations are easy places to observe rats because cats generally don't kill adult rats, while the heaps of food left out feed booming local rat populations.

Rats survive by avoiding notice, so focus your attention on sheltered paths to and from the food source. A rat will not run down the middle of the sidewalk, but the shadowed edge of the curb might be a rat highway. During daylight, keep an eye out for rat burrows near food sources as well as dead rats on city streets. However unfortunate we might find it that an animal got crushed by car tires, a dead rat is an undeniable indication of live rat activity. Come back at night, and you'll see the ones that crossed the road successfully.

WHERE: Sidewalks throughout the city

WHEN: Rats are active year-round, mostly at night.

EQUIPMENT: Wear whatever you do for a stroll down the sidewalk and bring a flashlight.

KIDS: The challenge for kids in observing rats is staying up late or getting up extremely early. That said, children have a keen eye for spotting small animals that adults tend to miss.

4

Winter Killers
Watch Cooper's and Sharp-Shinned Hawks

THE FLOCK OF PIGEONS had pulled into a tight ball as it flew above the cars and pedestrians on South Broad Street. They flew together across the street, and then the whole flock rippled and turned, flying back the way they had come. I paused on the sidewalk to watch them, and soon I spotted the bird that was not a pigeon. It flew above and then dove in, forcing the flock to deform and dodge. The pigeons changed direction and flew away, and it followed, looking for a tired straggler to pick off.

Every winter, two closely related hawks, Cooper's hawks and sharp-shinned hawks, move into Philadelphia to spend the colder months of the year eating our pigeons, starlings, and sparrows. Cooper's are larger than sharp-shinned hawks, but their plumage and shape are nearly identical. With females of both species being larger than males, there is an overlap in size between male Cooper's and female "sharpies."

You can spot these smaller hawks (compared to the ubiquitous red-tailed hawks) on tree branches or fences throughout the city and suburbs, waiting for an unwary bird to chase down in a high-speed burst of acrobatic flying.

They often hang out around bird feeders. Outside the city, they dodge tree trunks and blast through thickets after prey. Here, they fly under parked cars and turn tight corners around buildings in pursuit of smaller birds.

Adults of both species are gray with white-and-orange underparts. They have long tails marked with dark cross-bars. To make matters more confusing, the immature birds look a little like red-tailed hawks, with brown backs and dark streaks on their necks and chests. When in doubt, remember that the dark streaks of red-tailed hawks are concentrated in a band across their bellies and that red-tailed hawks are heftier birds with shorter tails.

Watch familiar birds like pigeons and crows (both similar in size to the hawks) year-round. Come winter, you will notice that some of the pigeon- or crow-sized birds have a different shape: longer tails and broader wings than pigeons, longer tails than crows. Also, watch starlings and sparrows making a commotion. They might be mobbing a hawk, trying to get it to move along before it has a chance to make a catch.

WHERE: You can watch these hawks everywhere, including in formal parks.

WHEN: Although a few Cooper's hawks breed in the city and are here in the summer, more show up toward the beginning of fall and stick around until spring.

EQUIPMENT: These birds are large enough to spot with the naked eye, but binoculars can help you observe them in more detail.

GUIDED VIEWING: Take a guided bird walk at a local park or nature center in fall and winter, and you just might encounter a Cooper's hawk or a sharp-shinned hawk with people who can point it out to you.

KIDS: The action can be unpredictable and quick, but when it happens, it provides the kind of drama that can easily excite children, even without binoculars.

5

Tree-Hugging
Give Some Love to Some Big Trees

ON A WALK IN HADDINGTON WOODS with the family, we found an enormous red oak tree toward the edge of the forest. To get a literal feel for the size of the tree, the three of us held hands to see whether we could get all the way around it. We couldn't. To me, the scale of the tree was apparent from the beginning, and I wasn't surprised. To my eight-year-old daughter, this tree-hugging attempt was an exercise in awe.

Sure, the term "tree hugger" gets thrown around as an insult, but let's embrace it. First of all, big trees are worth preserving for their carbon storage and local habitat function, serving as homes for owls, flying squirrels, and all sorts of other forest animals.

Also, actually touching and feeling the scale of something can make it more real to us. We talked about how old the enormous red oak must have been (two hundred years?) and just how old that was compared to human history. We talked about who must have been living there when the tree sprouted and how the rest of the forest, full of trees we could get our arms around, was so much younger by comparison.

Take a look at the shape of the tree as you size it up and hug it. Does its trunk reach straight up like a column and branch out only toward the top? If so, it probably grew in the shade of the forest and had to climb high early in its life. Does it have large branches lower down and a wider, gnarlier look to it? In that case, it probably grew on its own in a field, perhaps on a fence line or in a pasture, shading cows for a hundred years before the forest sprouted up around it.

If you're with kids, compare the big tree to the other trees you pass as you walk through the woods. Compare it to seedlings just sprouting in the underbrush, to saplings a few years older, to young skinny trees growing as fast as they can toward the sun shining through a gap in the canopy, and, finally, to the older, mature trees with trunks like columns.

WHERE: Haddington Woods is a section of Cobbs Creek Park north of Market Street, on the border of West Philadelphia and Delaware County.

ACCESS: The parking lot is where Vine Street dead-ends into the park. You can also enter the park just outside the 63rd Street El station. The trails are natural surface.

WHEN: You can hug trees at any time of year, but this is a good activity for winter, when there is less foliage to block your view.

FOR MORE INFORMATION: Additional information about big trees can be found at Champion Trees of Pennsylvania (http://www.pabigtrees .com/).

GUIDED VIEWING: The Cobbs Creek Community Environmental Center leads walks at Haddington Woods a few times per year.

OTHER LOCATIONS: There are plenty of big trees in other forests throughout the region. You can find some near you at Champion Trees of Pennsylvania (http://www.pabigtrees.com/). You can also nominate a large tree that isn't on the list and measure it yourself.

KIDS: I am sure that grown-ups can enjoy hugging trees on their own, but this is perfectly suited to kids of any age, particularly as a group activity for the whole family or whatever group is on the hike together. You can measure trees' circumferences with a measuring tape, or you can use hugs (this tree is one child's hug, the other takes the whole family, and so forth).

6

Tracing Their Steps
Track Animals in Snow, Mud, and Concrete

WE HAD GOTTEN LUCKY. I had planned to write an article about animal tracks in the snow, but it had been a warm winter so far, and photographer Christian Hunold and I needed the weather to cooperate. We needed snow—and not just any snow. We needed *wet* snow. For a novice like me, cold, dusty snow driven by the wind would have erased any prints immediately.

We awoke to find that mild snow showers the previous evening had left about an inch on the ground, all of it heavy and wet. We headed for the woods of Morris Park. I had my daughter, then a toddler, with me, and together, we followed the story of a red fox making its rounds along the banks of Indian Creek.

If you've got shallow, wet snow and good light (morning or late afternoon is best, with the lower angle of the sun casting better shadows in the prints), you'll be able to figure out most of the leading urban candidates pretty easily—for example, deer, opossums, raccoons, squirrels, as well as pets like dogs and cats. If you're not sure, measure the print and take a picture to compare it to prints you can find online or in a guide. Also, pay attention to the paths the prints take. Coyotes and foxes, for example, tend to walk in straighter lines than do dogs.

Snow is a beautiful medium for capturing animal prints, but mud also works. Check trails for prints made in muddy conditions. Drying sidewalk concrete preserves prints as well, and you can study dog, cat, squirrel, and other neighborhood animal prints with no worry that they'll melt away or erode the next time it rains.

WHERE: Morris Park offers easy trails through a mix of fields and forest. The park runs along the east and west branches of Indian Creek north of Haverford Avenue in the Overbrook Park neighborhood of West Philadelphia.

ACCESS: The park is open during daylight hours. Trailheads can be reached from Lansdowne Avenue and City Line Avenue (and buses running on those roads). Trails are gravel and natural surface.

WHEN: Whenever it snows or the rest of the year for prints set in mud and concrete

FOR MORE INFORMATION: Visit the Friends of Morris Park Facebook page. Images of the most common animal tracks are easy to find online. For more advanced tracking, consult a book, such as the *Peterson Field Guide to Animal Tracks*. iNaturalist has a "North American Animal Tracks Database" project, so upload photos of the prints you find for help in identifying them.

EQUIPMENT: A small ruler will come in handy for measuring prints. Wear shoes suitable for a light hike in snow.

GUIDED VIEWING: It is hard to plan a program around snow when it is so unpredictable, but the nearby Cobbs Creek Community Environmental Center and many other nature centers offer winter nature walks that, if there is snow on the ground, offer the opportunity to learn about animal signs from experts. Walks the rest of the year will take note of prints left in drying mud.

OTHER LOCATIONS: Any wooded park accessible early in the morning will work for this activity, but so will your garden, yard, or sidewalk.

KIDS: You might have to help smaller children work out the identifications, but they can enjoy the stories told or be inspired by the paths that animals took.

7

Dead Plant Time Machine
Explore an Herbarium Online

WE ARE NOT THE FIRST PEOPLE to explore nature here. Of course, we should start with the generations of indigenous peoples who inhabited what we now call Philadelphia. Then, during colonization, coinciding with modern European science's drive to catalogue everything under the sun, naturalists collected specimens and preserved them, with these collections often ending up in museums. Philadelphia was a hub of science and exploration in colonial North America and after the Revolution, meaning that the area has been well explored for centuries, and our museums have incredibly important collections of specimens.

With a few clicks, you can view these and more recent specimens online. I took a look at a cream violet[1] (*Viola striata*), a species I grow in my own native plant garden. This particular specimen was collected by Thomas C. Porter, a prominent Pennsylvania botanist. He found it in 1868 in Manayunk, a Philadelphia neighborhood I've spent my 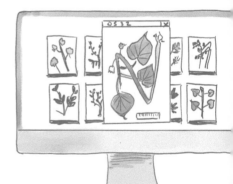 fair share of time in, whether riding my bike, hitting the local bars and restaurants, or watching turtles along the canal towpath. The violet specimen is dried and faded, but in my mind, I have an easy time brightening its pale green and straw tones to the deep green leaves and creamy white flowers that caught Porter's eye more than 150 years ago.

---

1. Mid-Atlantic Herbaria Consortium, accessed on October 29, 2020, https://midatlanticherbaria.org/portal/index.php.

Although the main purpose of this book is to get you outside to connect with nature, using all your senses, here is a way you can connect with nature and history at the same time, albeit indoors and through a screen. Advanced imaging and database technology have fueled a recent wave of digitization projects, in which museum specimens are scanned or photographed so that researchers can use them without traveling to view them in person or the museum having to ship them out.

Nonresearchers (i.e., the rest of us) can also peruse these images. These databases and websites are generally set up for academic researchers more than the general public, so their online search forms can take a little getting used to. Once you get the hang of it, though, you will find yourself immersed in hundreds of thousands of plants.

If you enjoy viewing herbarium specimens online and would like to pitch in, the digitization projects themselves could use your help. Modern technology can do a lot of things better than humans, but apparently reading human handwriting, or even notes typed by old typewriters, aren't some of them. You can volunteer to type notes on the specimen pages, helping make more museum records available online.

WHERE: This is an online activity.

WHEN: This is perfect for when you can't get outside or when you might not feel like it.

ACCESS: The Mid-Atlantic Herbaria Consortium's website (https://midatlanticherbaria.org/) is a good place to start. There, you can browse or search by species and look at photographs of live and preserved plants. You can also sign up to help digitize Mid-Atlantic's herbarium collections.

EQUIPMENT: All you need is a computer and a comfortable chair. Depending on the time of day, a cup of coffee or a nice cocktail can help.

KIDS: Children who enjoy exploring nature can connect to people like them who did the same activity in the past. Children will likely need help navigating the databases.

8

Cold Hands, Hot Birding
Take Part in a Winter Bird Count

WE STOOD AT THE EDGE of a city recycling yard in Northeast Philadelphia just after dawn, scanning the Delaware River for waterfowl and watching the edges of the industrial buildings around us for other birds. However cold we felt at that moment, the team of mid-winter bird census participants I was tagging along with was grateful for the warmth of the rising sun. They assured me that last year was much colder. We counted the waterfowl, an assortment of ducks as well as coots and Canada geese. We logged the fish crows and a raven we heard calling. An American kestrel landed on a smokestack behind us. We counted it too.

The National Audubon Society's Christmas Bird Counts evolved from Christmas bird shoots about a century ago, and they are one of the birding world's most popular traditions. In Philadelphia, the Delaware Valley Ornithological Club's (DVOC's) mid-winter bird census, started by local ornithologist Keith Russell, continues the tradition with some small tweaks (Audubon's Christmas Bird Counts survey birds in an area defined as a fifteen-mile radius around a central point, and the long, narrow shape of Philadelphia couldn't fit neatly in one count).

No matter how many nature documentaries you watch about winter life in the Rockies or in Canada—foxes diving into the snow to catch voles, the breath of musk oxen visible as icy vapor—it can be hard to drag yourself outside in the cold and dark of winter. Many of our animals (the ones that don't migrate, hibernate, or die) keep living interesting lives through the cold, though. A group event like a Christmas Bird Count can give you the structure and camaraderie you need to pull on the wool socks and get outside.

Counting birds in winter can be as simple as sitting on your porch with a mug of hot chocolate, but you can also join groups organized by the DVOC or local Audubon chapters. Of course, teaming up with local birders can help compensate for your inability to tell a fish crow from an American crow or a scaup from a canvasback when they're backlit by the rising sun, and it's a great way to hone your birding skills.

WHERE: Christmas Bird Counts cover most of our area. The Philadelphia mid-winter bird census takes place across the city.

ACCESS: Winter bird counts can be done in local green spaces as well as close to home.

WHEN: The Christmas Bird Count runs December 14 through January 5. The DVOC's mid-winter bird census runs for one day in January, typically about a week after the Christmas Bird Count.

FOR MORE INFORMATION: Check out the National Audubon Society's website (https://www.audubon.org/) for information about joining Christmas Bird Counts near you and visit the DVOC's website (https://dvoc.org) for more information about the mid-winter bird census.

EQUIPMENT: Dress for the cold and bring binoculars.

GUIDED VIEWING: These events are quite social. As you check in with the DVOC or your local Audubon chapter, you can find other birders to team up with.

KIDS: This activity involves standing out in the cold and watching small, distant birds through binoculars. It might be challenging for small children.

9

Guess Who?
Practice Tree Identification in Winter

LEAVES MAKE IDENTIFYING deciduous trees easy. Anyone who has seen the Canadian flag knows what a maple leaf looks like. The same probably goes for the deeply lobed oak leaves, and the compound leaves of ash or walnuts are a big help when you're trying to figure out what you're standing under. It's a lot harder in the winter.

All bare trees might look the same to you at first, but look again. Plenty of clues can help you make an identification. For example, the shaggy-looking, flaking bark on the upper branches of a white oak is nothing like the red oak's, which has ridges linking up to look a bit like ski runs down a mountain. On a finer scale, the twigs will show distinctive scars where last year's leaves attached, and next year's leaves will appear as buds that can also help you.

You can start with a tree guidebook and any tree you can find—perhaps street trees you already know. Take a close look at the red maple on the corner, observing the bark and any twigs you can reach.

A walk in the forest will give you plenty of trees to work with, of course, and it helps to choose a forest where the trees are labeled, such as the Native Woodland Walk at Tyler Arboretum. Each tree becomes an instructional example or a question in a quiz, depending which side of the tree you stand on.

Regardless of whether the tree is labeled, you can also cheat by using what's on the ground around you. Of course, leaves get blown about and mixed up, but if most of the leaves at the base of a mystery tree are silver maple leaves, that might be a good place to start. The same goes for the fruit of the tree. Do you see lots of acorns nearby or maybe the spiny husks of buckeyes? Up in the tree, you might find some dead leaves or fruit still hanging on that can help you out.

WHERE: Tyler Arboretum is in Delaware County.

ACCESS: The arboretum is best reached by car. It is open during the day and charges admission, so check the website for details about hours and costs. The Native Woodland Walk is natural surface.

WHEN: Winter

FOR MORE INFORMATION: Visit the arboretum's website (https://tylerarboretum.org).

EQUIPMENT: It's good to have a magnifying glass or a loupe to examine twigs. Wear shoes suitable for a light hike in the woods.

GUIDED VIEWING: Tyler Arboretum offers guided plant identification walks throughout the year, and volunteer docents can help guide you as you examine their trees.

OTHER LOCATIONS: Other arboretums and nature centers, including Morris Arboretum and the Schuylkill Center for Environmental Education, often offer winter plant identification walks. Arboretums in general label trees, and this includes those on some college campuses, such as the University of Pennsylvania's.

KIDS: Standing out in the cold and scrutinizing the finer features of trees might not appeal to young children, but they can help track down twigs and leaves. Older kids can get into solving the mystery of a tree's identity.

10

Roadkill Comes Alive
Search Roads by Bicycle for Dead Animals

WE HAD JUST WRAPPED UP a fruitless search for milk snakes, hours of hacking our way through the waist-high weeds of a power line cut in Northwest Philadelphia, when my friend took a call on his cell phone before getting into the car. Suddenly, his face perked up, and his eyes fixed on something on the pavement. He bent down and came up with a milk snake. This one had been dead for some time, and who-knows-how-many tires had flattened it into what herpers affectionately call "road jerky." It was not nearly as satisfying as finding a live snake, but we had nonetheless proven our hypothesis: Milk snakes indeed lived there.

"Road cruising" is a fundamental herping activity. You basically drive along roads through good habitat at night and hope something interesting chooses to cross in front of you. In the process, you also spot lots of dead-on-road (DOR) animals, all of them sad to see, but evidence nonetheless of species occurrence. Of course, reptiles and amphibians aren't alone in falling victim to cars and trucks. Anything that crawls, walks, runs, or even flies low to the ground can be found DOR as well.

Road cruising in a car doesn't make sense in urban or suburban landscapes the same way it does on long, open stretches of country blacktop. Nonetheless, urbanization is largely defined by how much of the landscape we have paved, and road mortality is one of the most powerful forces determining which animal species survive and which don't. Even the critters that adapt to crossing roads or manage to thrive in the small islands of green defined by our street grid sometimes fail to make it to the other side, and riding a bicycle along bike-safe streets or bike lanes is a great way to see what shares the neighborhood.

Roads through different habitat types will yield different species. You'll find squirrels and raccoons in our urban forests, rats in Center

City, and dead frogs and turtles next to ponds and wetlands, for example.

Keep one eye on traffic, of course, but also watch the pavement. Your eyes might be tricked by old banana peels, candy wrappers, ruptured dog-poop bags, and other trash, but you'll soon get used to spotting squashed squirrels, rats, toads, birds, and even some larger insects. Medium-sized animals, such as opossums, cats, and raccoons, are, of course, much easier to find. Take photos for reference and upload them to iNaturalist, where they can serve as important data points for future researchers, not just as sad reminders of the gory consequences of our society's addiction to motor vehicles.

EQUIPMENT: It's good to have a magnifying glass or a loupe to examine twigs. Wear shoes suitable for a light hike in the woods.

KIDS: Searching for roadkill from the sidewalk is suitable for children of all ages. Of course, exercise caution in having children ride bikes in the street.

11

Duck, Duck, Coot!
Observe Winter Waterfowl

ON A BIRDING WALK at the East Park Reservoir (now the site of the Discovery Center), I struggled to find the red-necked grebe the walk leader was so excited about. Grebes feed by catching fish underwater, which means that as I was trying to get a good look, the long-necked bird kept disappearing and then resurfacing somewhere else. It felt a bit like whack-a-mole with binoculars.

Every fall, we bid farewell to insect-eating songbirds that fly south to where they can still catch bugs. We then welcome northern waterfowl: ducks, geese, and other birds that need unfrozen water to float on and feed in. It doesn't seem to matter much to them whether that water is the Delaware River along the industrialized shoreline of Northeast Philadelphia, artificial ponds in FDR Park, or an old reservoir in North Philadelphia. This means that urbanites with a pair of binoculars can hop in their car, ride their bike, or take SEPTA to see animals usually regarded as symbols of the great, wild north of our continent.

Find a body of water and bring your binoculars. Shorelines in parks can be great places to bird, but so can more industrialized places, like old piers and reservoirs. Indeed, the Discovery Center (run in a collaboration between the National Audubon Society and Outward Bound) owes its existence to waterfowl that didn't care that the East Park Reservoir had been constructed for human drinking water. When the Audubon Society went looking for a site for an urban nature center, the birds pointed the way.

Not all waterfowl are looking for the same water, so you will find different species depending on where exactly you go. Smaller dabbling ducks, such as gadwall or blue-winged teal, might look for shallower, more sheltered water, like the marshy ponds at FDR Park or the impoundment at the John Heinz National Wildlife Refuge at Tinicum, whereas a larger diving duck, such as a greater scaup, will tend toward deeper water, like the Delaware River.

Consider the time of day and angle of the sun. Backlit waterfowl can just look like indistinguishable silhouettes, so having the sun behind you can make a huge difference.

WINTER

WHERE: The Discovery Center is in East Fairmount Park next to the Strawberry Mansion neighborhood in North Philadelphia, easily reached by car, public transportation, or human-powered means.

ACCESS: Entry to the Discovery Center grounds is free, and it is easy to reach by car or SEPTA. The center's paths are paved. The center has limited hours, so check the website before visiting.

WHEN: Winter

FOR MORE INFORMATION: Check out the Discovery Center's website (https://www.discoveryphila.org/) for more information.

EQUIPMENT: Although you can observe waterfowl with the naked eye, binoculars or spotting scopes are a huge help in making out details. Bundle up because you will end up standing still in some cold, windy spots.

GUIDED VIEWING: Birding walks through the winter target migratory waterfowl, so you can find guided programming at the Discovery Center as well as at parks and nature centers across the region. Also, check with the Delaware Valley Ornithological Club (DVOC) or your local Audubon chapter for walks near you.

OTHER LOCATIONS: Bodies of water throughout the region host winter waterfowl. The John Heinz National Wildlife Refuge at Tinicum, for example, offers guided walks as well as binoculars and guidebooks for visitors.

KIDS: If your child is old enough to use binoculars, this can be a fun winter activity.

12

Stump Yourself
Find Beaver Signs

THE FIRST TIME I WENT LOOKING for beaver-chewed stumps in Tacony Creek Park, I walked right past them. I had no excuse; I had interviewed a frustrated Water Department official about the row of newly planted oak trees the beaver had taken out, and he had given me perfectly good directions. What tricked me was that these were not the little saplings I had imagined. I suppose I had always known that beaver were capable of cutting down proper trees, but I was still impressed when Christian Hunold, who was photographing the damage for the article I was working on, pointed out the eight-inch stumps along the multiuse path, clear as day.

Beaver were wiped out in our area by fur trappers pretty early in European colonization. Twentieth-century reintroduction efforts reestablished them in Pennsylvania,[1] and from there they have spread into our urban waterways, where they give us a run for our money as landscape architects. We might decide that trees planted along waterways will be perfect to soak up rainwater and provide forest canopy, but the beaver might disagree, viewing them as foliage and bark for munching and wood for building.

You might think of beaver stacking tree branches across mountain streams to create ponds that they can swim in and in which they can build lodges. However, in waterways that are deep enough already and too wide to dam, they're just as likely to burrow into the muddy banks and forget construction.

You might be lucky enough to see a beaver swimming through the water or gathering vegetation at the shore, particularly at dawn and

---

1. Tom Hardisky, *Beaver Management in Pennsylvania (2010–2019)* (Harrisburg, PA: Pennsylvania Game Commission, 2011), accessed October 29, 2020, https://www.pgc .pa.gov/HuntTrap/TrappingandFurbearers/Documents/Beaver%20Management%20 in%20Pennsylvania%202010-2019.pdf.

WHERE: Look for Tacony Creek Park in North Philadelphia, particularly near where Rising Sun Avenue crosses the park.

ACCESS: There is a gateway (trailhead) to the park at Rising Sun Avenue, which can be reached by car or by SEPTA. The trail is paved.

WHEN: Beaver signs can be seen year-round.

FOR MORE INFORMATION: Check out the Tacony Creek Park Keepers' website (https://tcpkeepers.org/) to learn more about the park.

EQUIPMENT: Shoes and attire for light hikes along flat woodland trails will suffice.

GUIDED VIEWING: The Tookany/Tacony-Frankford Watershed Partnership offers nature walks and other programs in Tacony Creek Park.

OTHER LOCATIONS: Beaver live in most of our rivers and creeks, so keep an eye out along the floodplains wherever you hike. Beaver and their signs are particularly easy to observe at the mouth of the Pennypack at Pennypack on the Delaware and around the Impoundment at the John Heinz National Wildlife Refuge at Tinicum. You can also see a lodge at Silt Island (just above Fairmount Dam) on the Schuylkill from the other side of the river on MLK Drive.

KIDS: Hiking and looking for beaver-chewed stumps is great fun for children of all ages. Even if you don't see the animals themselves, it's fun to think about the powerful teeth it takes to chew through a tree.

dusk, but it's much easier to find trees they have been gnawing on and the stumps they leave behind. Beaver take trees down with their teeth, so you're looking for wood chewed away in bite-sized chunks rather than a flat-topped stump sawed off by a human or the jagged splinters left by a tree snapped off in a storm.

13

Tapping In
Make Maple Syrup

A FEW YEARS AGO, I got to try sycamore syrup. A friend had gotten on a syruping kick, and along with rigging maple trees with taps, tubing, and buckets, he had done the same with London plane trees (a variety of sycamore) along the street near his house in the Germantown neighborhood of Philadelphia. We tried it (along with maple syrup he also made) on pancakes, and it was delicious, with a little bit of a butterscotch flavor.

Of course, making syrup isn't just a way to enhance your breakfast—it's a window into how trees shift from winter dormancy into photosynthesis and growth. As temperatures warm, the tree starts sending nutrients—sugar being what we care about for syrup—up from the roots to fuel growth (flowers, seeds, leaves, and so forth) in the rest of the tree.

Although sugar maples have particularly sweet sap (meaning there is less boiling down to do), it turns out that other trees, such as sycamores and birches, produce sap that you can also turn into syrup.

Tapping a tree is as simple as driving a tap into the tree trunk and directing the sap into a bucket, either one hung beneath the tap or routed into by tubing. Timing is critical. You need temperatures rising above freezing during the day and dipping back below at night, usually from mid-February into early March.

Beware that the equipment and time investment involved in making your own syrup might be prohibitive. My syruping friend's production was shockingly low: after a winter of preparation and tapping and then many hours of boiling

down about fifteen gallons of sap, he was left with a couple of pints of syrup.

It is easiest to take part in the process at a local nature center. The Cobbs Creek Community Environmental Center in West Philadelphia holds a maple syrup event where you can learn about tree ecology and tapping and see sap being boiled down into syrup and maple sugar. Best of all, you can sample the product with next-to-no effort.

WHERE: The Cobbs Creek Community Environmental Center sits in Cobbs Creek Park in West Philadelphia.

ACCESS: The maple syrup event is free. The park is open year-round, from dusk till dawn. The area behind the center where the maple syrup event is held is paved. The center is not directly accessible by public transportation, but the 42 bus and the 34 trolley will get you to within a ten-minute walk on a paved path.

WHEN: The maple syrup event takes place in late February. Check the center's calendar on Facebook for the specific date.

FOR MORE INFORMATION: The Penn State Extension has free information for beginners about how to tap trees and make syrup. Visit the Cobbs Creek Community Environmental Center's Facebook page for information about the maple syrup event.

EQUIPMENT: To tap a tree for sap, you'll need a tap, a bucket, and a hook to hang it from.

OTHER LOCATIONS: Many nature centers and arboretums hold maple syrup events, including Tyler Arboretum.

KIDS: Have you ever had to bar your children from pouring their own syrup on their pancakes to keep them from flooding the table? Maple syrup is a great way to get a child's attention, hopefully teaching them something about tree biology and forest ecology in the process.

WINTER

II. Spring

14

Fleeting Beauties
Find Spring Ephemeral Wildflowers

No matter how hard I try, I can't make spring last all year. For me, it all seems to end once the forest canopy closes up. The temperature climbs, and the air grows heavier, more still. Shrubs leaf out as well, and the first wildflowers of the spring fade amid the shaded leaf litter.

The best I can do is get outside as much as possible and stretch the spring out through activity and attention. I might not be able to make the spring beauties keep their delicate pink-shaded white flowers open any longer, but I can make sure to see them. The same is true for a fleeting carpet of white bloodroot flowers and their fan-shaped, almost finger-lobed leaves and, of course, the trilliums, imposing with their three long petals held well above the leaf litter. These and several other species of woodland plants take advantage of the brief period of sunny warmth before the tree leaves high above them cut off the light.

It is not just the brevity of their bloom times that makes it challenging to enjoy these flowers. Their blanket of leaf litter is devoured and churned up by exotic earthworms, and overpopulated deer browse the native plants, giving the exotic, unpalatable plants the advantage. Those invaders include the lesser celandine, whose yellow buttercups carpet the floors of so many of our urban forests.

It takes active forest management and some luck to keep the spring ephemerals blooming, as they do at the Wildflower Loop at the Schuylkill Center for Environmental Education. The half-mile trail makes it easy: Simply walk slowly and pay attention to the forest floor around you.

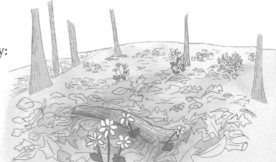

Also, look at slopes elsewhere on the grounds. You can find spring wildflowers where steep grades have made it difficult to grow crops over the centuries (leaving the forest soil intact and free of exotic earthworms), such as along Smith Run on the Ravine Trail. And, of course, keep coming back. The wildflowers do not all bloom at once, so you might see bloodroot on one walk and yellow trout lilies a few weeks later.

Tempting as it can be, do not pick any flowers. A plant that only has a few weeks to sprout, flower, and fruit doesn't recover well from trauma, and just a few years of having flowers or leaves damaged can be enough to kill a perennial plant that has been growing and blooming for decades.

WHERE: The Schuylkill Center is in Upper Roxborough in Philadelphia.

ACCESS: Trails at the Schuylkill Center are open from dusk till dawn, but the visitor center and front gate have more limited hours. Check the website for the current schedule. The trails are natural surface. The center is not directly accessible by SEPTA, but the 9 bus will get you to within a twenty-minute walk.

WHEN: Spring ephemeral wildflowers generally bloom from March into May.

FOR MORE INFORMATION: Visit the Schuylkill Center's website (https://www.schuylkillcenter.org).

EQUIPMENT: Dress for a walk in the woods on uneven trails.

GUIDED VIEWING: The Schuylkill Center offers guided wildflower tours as well as a self-guided tour of the Wildflower Loop.

OTHER LOCATIONS: Programming at other nature centers highlights spring ephemeral wildflowers, so check with your local center. A little farther afield, Bowman's Hill Wildflower Preserve features spring ephemerals as well.

KIDS: This is an easy and rewarding activity for children. The flowers are beautiful and easy to observe.

15

The Family That Preys Together
Watch Red-Tailed Hawks

NEW YORK CITY HAD ITS CELEBRITY red-tailed hawk, Pale Male, and for a while, we had Mom. This female red-tailed hawk spent a decade nesting along the Benjamin Franklin Parkway in Philadelphia, first attracting notice at her nest outside a window of the Franklin Institute. Like any self-respecting science museum, it put up a camera and shared the nesting scenes online.

Those images of nesting hawks sparked an online community of hawk watchers who tuned in to observe the family. Eventually, the online community shifted onto the ground,

photographing the hawks, blogging about them, and advocating for them. For example, after two fledglings died in window collisions, the hawk watchers encouraged the nearby Moore College of Art and Design to put up artwork that screens its windows, presenting a visual barrier to young hawks that don't understand glass. Mom was on her fourth mate and had fledged her twenty-fifth offspring on the

WHERE: The Benjamin Franklin Parkway in Center City, Philadelphia. Also, check online.

WHEN: The hawks nest from late winter into the spring, and the babies are usually fledging (leaving the nest) in June. The fledglings hang around into the summer and are relatively easy to observe. In general, they are most active right after sunrise.

FOR MORE INFORMATION: Visit the Franklin Hawkaholics Facebook page (https://www.facebook.com/groups/FranklinHawkaholics/).

EQUIPMENT: Although red-tailed hawks are usually visible to the naked eye, binoculars will help you observe the hawks in detail.

GUIDED VIEWING: Guided bird walks anywhere in the area are good opportunities to see red-tailed hawks. Once you know what to look for, you can search near your neighborhood.

OTHER LOCATIONS: Red-tailed hawks are ubiquitous urban birds. You probably have a pair nesting within a mile of wherever you live. Once you spot the adults, watch carefully in the spring to locate the nest.

KIDS: Kids of any age can enjoy the photos and videos of hawks, and as soon as they can handle a pair of binoculars, they'll find red-tailed hawks to be large, dramatic, and charismatic birds to observe IRL.

Parkway when she died in 2019.[1] Hawks continue to nest along the parkway, and the Franklin Hawkaholics still share their reports and images online.

Although the recent nests have not been in good positions for live streaming, a visit to the Franklin Hawkaholics Facebook page can still fill you in on the latest updates on the hawks, including photographs of them hunting, flying, and otherwise going about their business.

You can also visit the parkway with your binoculars to watch them yourself, and the existing community of hawk watchers makes it relatively easy to find the hawks and learn their habits.

---

1. Pamela Dimeler, "Mom, in 2017," Facebook, March 21, 2019, https://www.facebook.com/groups/FranklinHawkaholics/permalink/10156472203392029.

16

Amphibian Crossing Guards
Help the Toad Cross the Road

HERPERS LIKE ME pay a lot of attention to the blacktop. Reptiles and amphibians are often easy to encounter crossing the road, and even those that fall victim to crushing tires provide evidence that others can be found nearby. Nonetheless, we root for the critters against the cars. When we find a stretch of road littered with squashed carcasses, we wish someone would shut it down or do something else to protect the critters. Imagine my delight in 2009 when similarly concerned neighbors teamed up with the Schuylkill Center for Environmental Education to help the American toads that breed in the Upper Roxborough Reservoir by closing Port Royal Avenue during toad-breeding season.

American toads are common woodland critters in our area, snapping up worms and bugs and regarding their leaf-litter world with heavy brows and a wide-mouthed frown. Come springtime, the male toads hop their way to the nearest slow body of water, stake their claim to a muddy patch, and start singing their musical trill to attract the females. Once they're done, they return to their woodland territories and leave their long strings of black eggs behind to hatch into tadpoles.

The Upper Roxborough Reservoir, long abandoned to weeds and wildlife, is a perfect breeding spot for the toads of the Schuylkill Center's grounds, just across Port Royal Road. On rainy nights in March and April, when the toads migrate over to the reservoir (and a few weeks later, head back), the Schuylkill Center's Toad Detour program shuts down Port Royal to car traffic and outfits volunteers with reflective vests to usher the toads across the road.

WHERE: The Roxborough Reservoir is in the Upper Roxborough neighborhood of Northwest Philadelphia.

ACCESS: Follow the Toad Detour organizers' parking instructions. The 9 bus gets you a block away from the reservoir.

WHEN: American toads breed in mid-spring, but the exact timing depends on rainfall and temperatures and can vary from year to year.

FOR MORE INFORMATION: Contact the Schuylkill Center for Environmental Education (https://www.schuylkillcenter.org) for general information about the Toad Detour as well as the best way to learn about the nights when the toads are moving.

EQUIPMENT: Bring a flashlight and, because the toads will often move in the rain, clothes you don't mind getting wet.

GUIDED VIEWING: The Toad Detour is a carefully overseen event. You will undergo a short orientation before you head out onto the road to help the toads, guided by experienced staff and volunteers.

OTHER LOCATIONS: Spring amphibian road-crossing projects are becoming more popular, so check with nature centers near you. French Creek State Park, for example, offers programming to observe breeding frogs and salamanders in early spring.

KIDS: American toads' slow pace makes them easy for children to catch and examine. The Toad Detour in Roxborough is set up for children to take part and even practice at being citizen scientists, wielding pencils and clipboards as they tally the toads they've helped across the road. It is safest for the toads—as well as for kids young enough to consider putting toads in their mouths—to use a jar or a cup to hold toads as you move and examine them.

17

Feathered Fallout
Watch Spring Songbird Migration

BIRDERS, LIKE ANY OTHER COMMUNITY of naturalists, employ some funny lingo. My favorite term of all is the "warbler fallout." In mid-spring, usually toward the end of April and heating up into May, these songbirds that wintered to the south—anywhere from the Southeast of the United States down to Brazil—fly north again. Some are coming back to our area to nest, but many are continuing north to the forests, fields, and wetlands that stretch up the Appalachians and into Canada. Many of them travel together in flocks by night, covering a couple hundred miles or so, and then land in the morning to refuel on any bugs they can catch. When a flock touches down where you happen to be birding, it can seem like every tree and shrub is alive with small, colorful birds singing as they dart in and out after every caterpillar, moth, and spider they can find.

Philadelphia sits along the Atlantic Flyway, sort of a migration superhighway up the Atlantic Coast. That means that almost any park with good tree cover can host dozens of species of birds over the course of a few weeks. Awbury Arboretum in Germantown is one of those parks, with birders logging upwards of fifty species of birds in a single visit in May.

Awbury Arboretum has embraced its birding hotspot status by hosting birding events, participating in Philly bird censuses, and offering field studies programs for children to learn about birds. The arboretum also posts a "bird board" so that visitors can see what others are spotting.

Simply pointing your binoculars at small birds in trees will yield some interesting observations in the spring, but with a little technique, you can spot a lot more. Be sure to search for moving birds with the naked eye. Many of these are quite small, smaller than a house sparrow. Once you spot the target bird, raise the binoculars into position as you keep your eyes locked on the bird. Also, listen. This is a great time for birding by ear. Male (mostly) birds often sing as they forage for bugs.

Birders are often quite social, so feel free to politely ask what someone is watching, and then see whether you can spot it yourself. This is a great way to hone your bird identification skills as well.

WHERE: Awbury Arboretum is in the East Germantown area of Philadelphia.

ACCESS: Awbury's grounds are open dawn to dusk through the year. It has one paved trail; others are natural surfaces. Awbury can be reached by buses on Chew Avenue as well as the Washington Lane regional rail stop.

WHEN: Spring songbird migration peaks from late April into late May.

FOR MORE INFORMATION: Visit Awbury Arboretum's website (https://awbury.org).

EQUIPMENT: To see birds, bring binoculars. They'll be small and far away.

GUIDED VIEWING: Check Awbury's events calendar for guided birding. You can learn birding basics with programs like BirdPhilly's guided walks (learn more at https://birdphilly.org) and Birding Backpacks that you can check out of your local library.

OTHER LOCATIONS: Birding walks take place during the spring at pretty much every park and nature center. Major hotspots include Carpenter's Woods and the John Heinz National Wildlife Refuge at Tinicum, but check with a center or park near you. You can also view migrants in pocket parks and in trees in your neighborhood. The birds head for green spaces, regardless of whether they are officially parks.

KIDS: Watching and listening to birds is suitable for kids of all ages, but they will enjoy it more as they learn to use binoculars. Kids might also enjoy keeping a list of what they've seen.

18

A Trilling Adventure
Join a Frog Call Survey

FEW SOUNDS IN NATURE are as loud and all-encompassing as a chorus of spring peepers. The frogs are about the size of your thumbnail, but the high-pitched sound they make is huge. Coming at the end of the bleak, gray cold of winter, the enveloping wall of frog calls heralds the return of life. Spring is here.

Of course, frogs call for their own benefit, not ours. Those peepers have emerged from winter dormancy (in some cases, quite literally frozen solid; peepers are one of the frog species able to survive freezing) and have only mating on their minds. Males set up territory in a particularly promising clump of dead vegetation and call as loudly as they can to attract females.

There is no missing their song, but the frogs themselves otherwise do their best to avoid notice. Thus, their calls are the easiest way to tell whether they are there. This is true of most frogs and toads, for that matter: You have to be within a few feet to see one, but you might hear it calling from a hundred yards away. Moreover, some frogs can look pretty similar to human eyes, although their distinct calls make clear that they are different species. The mid-Atlantic leopard frog, which is found at the John Heinz National Wildlife Refuge at Tinicum, was described as a new species in 2014, aided by the distinctiveness of its call compared to that of the look-alike southern leopard frog.[1]

Researchers have used frog call surveys (although they also survey for toads, the surveys are generally referred to as just "frog call survey") for decades as a way to learn more about

---

1. J. A. Feinberg et al., "Cryptic Diversity in Metropolis: Confirmation of a New Leopard Frog Species (Anura: Ranidae) from New York City and Surrounding Atlantic Coast Regions," *PLOS ONE* 9, no. 10 (October 2014), doi:10.1371/journal.pone.0108213.

WHERE: The John Heinz National Wildlife Refuge at Tinicum

ACCESS: The refuge is not usually open after dusk, so be sure to sign up for the frog call walks. The paths at the refuge are either gravel or natural surface. It is not directly accessibly by public transportation but is about a five-minute walk from bus stops at 84th Street and Lindbergh Boulevard.

WHEN: Frog-monitoring walks run in the spring.

FOR MORE INFORMATION: Start checking the refuge's Facebook page in early March for more information about the walks.

EQUIPMENT: Wear shoes suitable for flat, gravel trails and dress warmly enough for cool spring evenings. Bring a flashlight, but the less you use it, the better you'll preserve your night vision.

OTHER LOCATIONS: Parks and nature centers often offer nighttime amphibian programming, so check with a center near you. French Creek State Park, for example, offers programming to observe breeding frogs and salamanders early in the spring.

KIDS: Attending a frog call survey is fun for kids old enough to stay up well after dark, but younger children can enjoy frog calls heard during the daytime, particularly in cloudy or wet weather.

where they live and how many there are. Repeated the same way year after year, these observations can tell us about population trends and the need for conservation interventions. The human participants head out at night and stop at predetermined locations. There, they note the weather conditions, listen to the calls, and then write down what species they're hearing and how big the chorus is.

Of course, it is important to be able to differentiate types of frog calls. Taking part in a frog call survey led by experienced observers is a great way to learn. The John Heinz National Wildlife Refuge at Tinicum partners with the Philadelphia Zoo to monitor the frogs of the refuge. You can take part in evening walks there, get the hang of observing calling frogs, and immerse yourself in the sounds of spring.

19

Scales and All
Flip Brown Snakes

MANY YEARS AGO, a neighbor asked me to identify a foot-long, tan-colored snake her cat had dragged in (the fifth snake, actually, but the first four had died). I knew it immediately as a brown snake, also sometimes called a DeKay's snake, a completely innocuous species that eats slugs and worms. I was a little surprised to hear that at least five of them were living, or at least had been, on a West Philly block of old three-story twin houses. Along with kindling a profound frustration with people who let their cats go outside, this event drew my attention to searching for snakes in urban landscapes.

I started looking under rocks, logs, or trash (an activity called "flipping," as in flipping boards or flipping rocks) not just in parks but in friends' backyards, in vacant lots, along railroad tracks—basically, anywhere with a little vegetation and something for a small snake to hide under. And, in many of the places I looked, I found them.

An old board or a rock can be a shield against predators, such as robins or raccoons. It can transmit the heat of the sun, and it can help retain moisture in dry weather. By looking underneath, you can find brown snakes as well as myriad other animals that hide during the day.

As simple as this activity is, you must follow a few key rules to stay safe and avoid injuring the snakes or ruining their habitat:

- Use a tool, such as a garden hoe or a cultivator, to grip boards with nails sticking out of them or other sharp-edged objects.
- Always replace the object exactly how you found it so it can continue serving as shelter.
- Release the snakes *after* you replace the cover object to avoid crushing them. They will find their way back underneath. If you aren't picking up the snakes, gently scoot them out of the way.
- Never lift something too heavy for you to control with one

arm. Otherwise, as you are trying to hold the object up with one hand while reaching under with the other, you could lose your grip and smash the critters underneath.

Brown snakes are the easiest snake species to find in urban settings, but you might turn up others, particularly garter snakes. They might bite, but they are not venomous, so the most they can do is leave you with some scratches. Venomous snakes live in the Pine Barrens of New Jersey (timber rattlesnakes) and in the outer fringes of Bucks, Chester, and Montgomery Counties (copperheads), virtually all beyond the range of this urban guide. When in doubt, don't pick it up.

WHERE: Gardens, vacant lots, railroad tracks, and the weedy edges of cemeteries and manicured parks are all great places to look for brown snakes.

WHEN: Brown snakes are easiest to find when temperatures are in the sixties and above.

EQUIPMENT: A tool, such as a hoe or cultivator, for gripping sharp objects will come in handy. So will a rag for cleanup. Brown snakes defend themselves by pooping and releasing a stinky musk.

GUIDED VIEWING: Local nature centers occasionally offer snake-themed walks.

KIDS: This is a fun activity for children, but adult supervision is important when judging safe places to search, lifting heavy and sometimes sharp objects, and taking care with delicate creatures. Brown snakes, although cute, generally do poorly in captivity, so resist the "Can I take it home, *PLEASE*?" requests.

20

Cheep Thrills
Bird by Ear

SOMETIMES, I BIRD FROM THE BEDROOM. As I'm waking up on spring or summer mornings and trying to muster the will to sling myself out of bed, I listen to the birds outside the window. Mockingbirds will sing, imitating phoebes, gulls, and various other birds that they must have heard somewhere else. Cardinals will move through with their metallic chip notes, and, of course, the sparrows "cheep" incessantly.

Most birds are noisy creatures. They sing or call to attract mates and defend territory. A variety of other calls helps them keep track of each other—think of geese honking as they fly through the sky in V-formation. Alarm calls notify neighbors of threats, such as house cats or hawks. Indeed, chickadees are named for their "chick-a-dee-dee-dee" scolding call.

Listening to birds can be as productive as looking for them. Frequently, the twittering of chimney swifts announces their presence high above the rooftops. A ruckus of scolding songbirds can signal that a hawk or an owl is near. You might not spot a nighthawk in the dimming light at the end of the day, but its "peent" calls tell you it's up there somewhere. Many species stay out of sight but sing or call back and forth with little chip notes as they move through trees and bushes. If your goal is visually observing birds, learning their sounds is a great way to locate and identify them.

For people with visual impairments,[1] birding by ear can open the

---

1. Trevor Attenberg, "Birding Blind: Open Your Ears to the Amazing World of Bird Sounds," Audubon, October 18, 2018, accessed October 29, 2020, https://www.audubon.org/news/birding-blind-open-your-ears-amazing-world-bird-sounds.

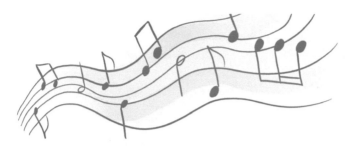

natural world to observation and enjoyment. You don't need to see birds to know what they're doing.

There are a lot of ways to learn to bird by ear. If you can see birds, matching the birds you see with their sounds can help you identify them the next time you hear them. Audubon's library of bird songs is available on smart speakers, for example, and multiple bird song quizzes online can help you learn, as can apps that can identify recorded bird calls.

GUIDED LISTENING: You can learn birding basics, including birding by ear, with such programs as BirdPhilly's guided walks (learn more at https://birdphilly.org). Although birding programming tends to be focused on seeing birds, the Cobbs Creek Community Environmental Center has partnered with Philly Touch Tours to offer birding programs focusing on bird songs as well as preserved birds that can be touched. Also, the Pennsylvania Center for Adapted Sports sponsors an Adapted Birding program for people with disabilities, including low vision and blindness.

FOR MORE INFORMATION: Learn more about the Cobbs Creek Community Environmental Center and its schedule of programming on its Facebook page (https://www.facebook.com/CobbsEnvCenter/). Learn more about Adapted Birding at the Pennsylvania Center for Adapted Sports's website (https://www.centeronline.com/). You can find a lot of birding-by-ear resources online—for example, at Audubon's website (https://www.audubon.org/birding-by-ear).

KIDS: Kids often can key in on bird sounds before they have an easy time spotting them by sight. My daughter Gilda, at twenty months old, spontaneously began imitating American crows in our neighborhood, "caw, caw, caw." Your kids are probably already familiar with the cawing of crows or the cheeping of house sparrows.

21

Weeds to Watch
Find Philadelphia Fleabane

CARL LINNAEUS DID NOT INTEND to honor the City of Brotherly Love when he named a species of daisy after the city. He was working in Sweden with plant samples sent to him by European naturalists in North America, and he used Philadelphia to indicate the broader area they were exploring.[1]

But who cares! We have a beautiful native wildflower named the Philadelphia fleabane (*Erigeron philadelphicus*), and it grows all over our city. Let's celebrate it.

The Philadelphia fleabane flowers from late April into May, opening its nickel-sized flower heads (white or pink rays with a yellow center) two or three feet above the ground.

The "ground" where the Philadelphia fleabane grows is just about anywhere it can find disturbed soil or a comfortable crack in the sidewalk. Given that the plant grows without human intervention, many homeowners and gardeners might consider it to be a weed, but you don't have to agree. To find them, simply walk around your neighborhood and look in unkempt yards, vacant lots, sidewalks,

---

1. Gerry Moore, "An Overview of Scientific Names Honoring the City of Philadelphia, Pennsylvania, with an Emphasis on Flowering Plants," *Bartonia*, no. 69 (2016): 90–117, accessed May 27, 2020, https://www.jstor.org/stable/44089931.

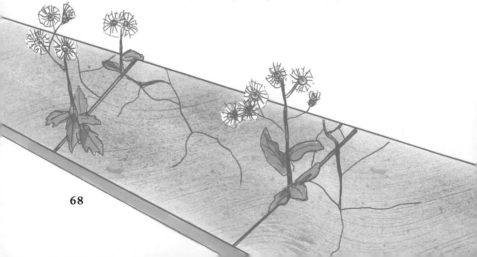

or anywhere else that hasn't been mowed or weeded. Other related species grow a little later in the spring and into the summer, but if you're looking in late April or early May, you're probably looking at a Philadelphia fleabane. If you're still unsure, check the leaves. The base of Philadelphia fleabane leaves "clasp" the stem, meaning that they wrap around rather than being set off by a petiole, which is the little stalk that you often find at the base of a leaf.

Once you find them, you can intentionally cultivate them if you would like them in your own garden. You can wait until the pollinated flower heads dry up and release their fluffy seeds (like those of a dandelion, but smaller) and then scatter them where you'd like. It is slightly more reliable to transplant fleabane that is growing where another gardener or landowner doesn't want them to grow. Once the flowering stalks have died back in the summer, note the location of the clumps of leaves at the base (basal leaves). In the fall, dig them up and plant them where you want them to grow.

WHERE: Nearly anywhere in the region

ACCESS: Philadelphia fleabane frequently grows in easy viewing range of sidewalks.

WHEN: Late April through May

EQUIPMENT: Philadelphia fleabane is easy to appreciate with the naked eye, but a magnifying glass can help you examine the flowers and any insect visitors stopping by for some pollen and nectar.

GUIDED VIEWING: The Philadelphia Botanical Club occasionally offers urban plant walks. Philadelphia fleabane also grows in more "natural" settings, so spring plant walks are also good opportunities to see and learn about them.

KIDS: Neighborhood plant hunts are a great way to get kids into botany and nature more generally. And although kids might have to be careful with rarer plants growing in parks, picking a Philadelphia fleabane from the edge of the sidewalk is probably fine. Ask the property owner to be safe, but they'll probably say yes and thank you for removing what they count as a weed. They might even let you dig it out by the roots so you can transplant it into your own garden.

22
Get on the Ball
Watch Water Snakes

"GIANT BALL OF SNAKES!" People like me who love snakes often field alarmed queries in late spring, when friends who have been hiking near water see what looks like a pile of snakes squirming and writhing on the shore. We patiently explain that love is in the air: what they've seen are northern water snakes mating. The much larger female attracts the attention of one or more of the smaller males, who all sort of wrestle with each other around her for the prize of getting to mate. As the year progresses through the summer, some of the same spots will host water snakes basking in the sun as they take a break from hunting fish and frogs.

At the edge of the Wissahickon Creek, right by the popular and historic Valley Green Inn, water snakes gather in the spring and early summer, sometimes freaking out the park visitors there to feed the ducks or start a hike.

Water snakes spend the winter hibernating in holes, out of sight and below the frost line. As the air and ground warm, they emerge to feed and seek a mate. In our area, they tend to be easiest to spot looking for love from May into June.

After that, they like to soak up the summer sun, particularly in the morning, as they get their body temperatures up above the cooler air and water. Any open spot with easy access to the water (for a quick getaway) will do. Water snakes often bask on low tree or bush branches over the water and drop off when startled, which leads to the occasional snake-in-a-canoe surprise.

At the end of the summer, water snakes give birth, and you might even get lucky and spot baby water snakes crawling around.

It is tempting to pick up the water snakes. Please remember that although they are not venomous, they do defend themselves with sharp, needlelike teeth. Their other end is also fierce, ejecting copious feces and musk; the smell will linger long after the encounter.

WHERE: Valley Green Inn is on Forbidden Drive in the Wissahickon Valley section of Fairmount Park in Northwest Philadelphia.

ACCESS: You can drive to the Valley Green Inn, but parking can be tight. You can also reach the inn on several Wissahickon Valley trails: Forbidden Drive, the Yellow Trail, and the Orange Trail. The outdoor areas are gravel.

WHEN: Late spring through summer

FOR MORE INFORMATION: Visit the Friends of the Wissahickon website (https://fow.org) for more information on the Wissahickon and for a schedule of walks and other events.

EQUIPMENT: Wear shoes suitable for hiking on sometimes-muddy trails.

GUIDED VIEWING: Few programs deal with water snakes specifically, but Friends of the Wissahickon offers more general nature walks that could provide good opportunities to spot water snakes.

OTHER LOCATIONS: Water snakes are common along our waterways. They are a little skittish, but if you see one slip away before you can get a good look, come back a little later and search from a little farther away so you don't spook them. You can also search under rocks and logs near the shore to find hiding water snakes.

KIDS: Watching snakes bask and go about their business is fun and accessible for kids. It's also a way to demystify snakes and cultivate appreciation rather than fear.

23

Join the Crowd
Take Part in a Bioblitz

I USUALLY LOOK UNDER LOGS for snakes and salamanders by myself ("flipping" logs, in herper lingo). On a walk through Bartram's Garden in late April 2019, though, I was joined by a small group of other nature enthusiasts, and I saw way more than I ever would have on my own. Someone pointed out the chocolate slime mold I had ignored. An entomologist in the group was quick to identify the beetles that I usually shuffle aside in my drive to find reptiles and amphibians. We found several horned passalus, large black beetles that eat rotting wood and raise their young in family groups—all of which I wouldn't have learned on my own.

The group was taking part in the City Nature Challenge, an international, competitive bioblitz in which cities compete to get the most people making the most observations of the most species in a four-day period. Bioblitzes are events in which a group of biologists with a variety of expertise (entomology, botany, herpetology, mycology, and so forth) try to catalog every living thing in a particular place, usually in a short period of time. They have become popular as well as events to engage the public in nature. Nature centers, parks, and watershed organizations hold bioblitzes to gather information about the local biodiversity as well as to get visitors excited about nature.

Experiencing nature alone has its benefits and pleasures, but one of the great things about exploring nature in a city is the option to do it socially. And, as satisfying as it is to wade into the guidebooks or keys to identify something yourself, it's a heck of a lot more efficient to have an expert next to you do it quickly.

Some bioblitzes are held as group events, where you'll show up as a volunteer or participant and experts will guide you as you observe

ACCESS: You can take part in a decentralized bioblitz like the City Nature Challenge or the TTF's fall bioblitz anywhere in the defined geographic area, whether that's in a wooded park space with rugged trails or right outside your home. Observation documentation can be in the form of photos or audio recordings (for example, for bird or frog calls).

WHEN: The City Nature Challenge takes place every spring for four days. The dates vary from year to year.

FOR MORE INFORMATION: Visit the main City Nature Challenge's website (https://citynaturechallenge.org) or the Philadelphia-specific website (https://cncphilly.org) to get the most up-to-date information on how to take part in the City Nature Challenge. Visit the TTF's website (https://ttfwatershed.org) to view its calendar and learn more about upcoming events.

OTHER LOCATIONS: Many parks, nature centers, and other green spaces hold bioblitzes, so check the calendars for a centralized bioblitz near you.

KIDS: These are great events to get kids hooked on nature. Bioblitzes lend themselves to contests or games. Group bioblitz events, with someone always finding something, provide a lot of action for kids with short attention spans.

and try to identify plants, animals, fungi, and even slime molds.

Other bioblitzes are more decentralized, often using a citizen science platform like iNaturalist to aggregate finds and conduct much of the hard work of identification online. The Tookany/Tacony-Frankford Watershed Partnership (TTF) holds a fall bioblitz for the watershed, for example, and, of course, the City Nature Challenge does something similar for Philadelphia and surrounding counties. Decentralized bioblitzes like these offer guided nature walks and other events for those who don't want to go it alone. For beginners and old hands alike, group events facilitate observation and identification and offer social interaction before sending participants off to continue on their own.

24

Falcons for Dinner
Watch Peregrine Falcons While You Eat

A COUPLE OF FRIENDS AND I had set up a spotting scope on the sidewalk next to the Couch Tomato Cafe and Bistro in Manayunk. We were there to observe the peregrine falcons that nest at St. John the Baptist Catholic Church.

It took only a couple of minutes for neighbors and passersby to chat us up about the birds. Some had been watching the falcons for years and shared their own observations. Other people hadn't realized that falcons were raising a family right overhead. Everyone enjoyed a peek through the spotting scope. After a little while, we sat down for dinner.

Peregrine falcons are the fastest animal alive, knocking their bird prey out of the sky with two-hundred-mile-per-hour dives. They were wiped out in Eastern North America by the pesticide DDT in the mid-twentieth century. The United States banned DDT in 1972, and in the following decades, conservation agencies transplanted falcons to places where they had been extirpated. Although the rocky cliffs they evolved to nest on are in short supply in the Philadelphia area, artificial cliffs (ledges on buildings and bridges) work just as well.

The steeple of St. John the Baptist Catholic Church in Manayunk offers just such a clifflike ledge as well as a commanding view of the cityscape and Schuylkill River below, perfect for spotting pigeons and other tasty birds. For those of us looking up, the Couch Tomato Cafe provides a good view of the church. Its sidewalk seating offers a great way to relax and study wildlife at the same time.

Once you're comfortable, look for a medium-sized raptor with pointy wings. Listen also for their harsh, high-pitched calls. Check ledges on the church steeple as well as on other structures for resting birds. As spring shifts into summer, the fledgling chicks leave the nest. They tend to hang out in the neighborhood, and you can often spot one or both of the parents catering to their offspring, which nag them for food.

WHERE: The Couch Tomato Cafe is at 100 Rector St. in Philadelphia's Manayunk neighborhood.

ACCESS: Check the cafe's website for its current hours, but if you're there earlier or if the weather isn't right for dining outside, the falcons are easy to spot from the sidewalks on Rector Street or from Venice Island, a park space nearby. The cafe is easily reached by buses along Main Street.

WHEN: The falcons nest in spring and hang out with their fledglings into the middle of summer.

FOR MORE INFORMATION: Visit the cafe's website (https://www.thecouchtomato.com) for information about the Couch Tomato.

EQUIPMENT: You can spot the peregrine falcons with the naked eye, but binoculars or a spotting scope will make it possible to observe them in detail.

GUIDED VIEWING: The Delaware Valley Ornithological Club (DVOC) holds an annual meetup at the Couch Tomato to watch the falcons in June.

OTHER LOCATIONS: Peregrine falcons nest in other viewable spots around the region—for example, at St. Cyprian Catholic Church off the Cobbs Creek Parkway, on bridges over the Delaware River, and, most famously, at Philadelphia City Hall.

KIDS: This is a good activity for children old enough to use binoculars. Of course, they'll skip the beer at the cafe, but they might still enjoy a slice of pizza while watching the falcons.

25

Sunbathing in Armor
Watch Basking Turtles

Iɴ ᴀ ᴄɪᴛʏ, ᴛʜᴇʀᴇ ɪꜱ ɴᴏ ᴡᴀʏ to separate natural history from human history. Nowhere is this more true but harder to observe than in our wetlands. The Delaware River estuary was originally lined by a vast network of marshes, most of which have been drained and filled in to create dry land. Where marshes currently exist, they have often been re-created or have filled in the gaps in the built environment, such as at the moat of Fort Mifflin. What was originally a barrier to invading troops is now full of spatterdock and other marsh vegetation and is alive with fish, frogs, turtles, and other wildlife.

I bet that neither the British, who built a fortification on "Mud Island" before the Revolutionary War, nor the Americans who fought from the fort during the war[1] intended their fort walls to be wildlife-viewing walkways. Nonetheless, when I visit Fort Mifflin, I bring my binoculars and take a close look at the turtles basking along the sides of the moat.

Turtles survive encounters with humans by getting into the water as fast as possible. Thus, the challenge of observing them basking is getting a good look before they see you looking at them. This is easiest in places with lots of human foot traffic, so that turtles have gotten used to all the people nearby.

At Fort Mifflin, you, like dozens of people every day that the moat's turtles have learned to ignore, can walk along the top of the fort walls. Unlike most of those other fort walkers, you can peer down at native species, such as the Pennsylvania-threatened red-bellied turtle (sometimes called a cooter) and painted turtles as well as the nonnative red-eared sliders, which are descendants of released pets. These turtles might be relatively unwary, but they will still notice

---

1. "The History of Fort Mifflin," Fort Mifflin, accessed October 29, 2020, http://www.fortmifflin.us/the-history/.

a human doing something unusual, like stopping and looking at them. So, try to observe them from as far away as possible. Binoculars will help keep you sufficiently distant to keep the turtles comfortable.

Also in the moat, you can spot stinkpots (aka common musk turtles) walking along the bottom. These small turtles bask less often than other species.

WHERE: Fort Mifflin is in the far southwest corner of Philadelphia, near the airport.

ACCESS: Fort Mifflin charges admission and is open to the public March 1 through December 15, Wednesday through Sunday, 10 A.M. to 4 P.M. The paths are often muddy, and observing the turtles requires a climb up steps to the top of the ramparts. Fort Mifflin has parking but is not accessible by public transit.

WHEN: Turtles will bask from spring into the fall. However, as the vegetation in the moat gets thick in the summer, it becomes harder to spot turtles, so spring is best.

EQUIPMENT: Dress for a light hike and bring binoculars for the best looks at the turtles.

OTHER LOCATIONS: Turtles are easy to spot basking in many bodies of water—for example, from the boardwalk at the John Heinz National Wildlife Refuge at Tinicum or at the mouth of Pennypack Creek at Pennypack on the Delaware.

KIDS: This activity is best suited to children old enough to use binoculars or a scope.

26

Dog Vomit Is Just the Beginning
Slime Mold Search

DOG VOMIT SLIME MOLD has one of the best names in all of nature. It is evocative and accurate. I was on a group walk along the Baxter Trail that crosses the mouth of Pennypack Creek and continues north along the Delaware when I spotted what looked like a bright yellow splatter just off the trail. However much it appeared to have been ejected there, we were actually looking at single-celled organisms, kind of like amoebas, that had pulled together into one mass. Previously, they had been living as individuals in the soil and leaf litter, and now they were one entity. If I had come back in a couple of days, I might have found the slime mold drying up a bit and releasing spores that could disperse and start the cycle all over again.

Our soil is teeming with microscopic life that we rarely get to witness directly, from tiny worms on down to bacteria. Tiny these creatures may be, but they play critical roles in cycling nutrients through the ecosystem and supporting the bigger life-forms we pay more attention to, such as trees. Slime molds, although not necessarily all related to each other, do us the unusual favor of pulling their tiny selves out of microscopic anonymity and taking on obvious forms, such as the yellow splatter of dog vomit, the bright pink bubbly lumps of raspberry slime mold, the pale blobs of wolf's milk, or the shaggy chocolate tube slime mold.

You can find slime molds by searching the ground and looking around rotting logs, particularly in moist wooded areas. Damp weather will be more productive than dry. Be sure to roll dead logs and peek under bark as you go (see tips for flipping logs in the "Scales and All: Flip Brown Snakes" entry). They are easily mistaken for fungi, so often your local mushroom hunters will be your best guides.

WHERE: The Baxter Trail, along the Delaware River in Northeast Philadelphia

ACCESS: The Baxter Trail is paved and can be reached from where it crosses Pennypack Street to the north or from Pennypack on the Delaware to the south. You can access Pennypack on the Delaware by the Holmesburg Junction Station. You can access both ends from buses along State Road.

WHEN: The Baxter Trail is open Memorial Day to Labor Day, 8 A.M. to 8 P.M. If you're visiting and find the Baxter Trail closed, the woods below the mouth of the Pennypack are also wonderful to explore.

FOR MORE INFORMATION: Visit Riverfront North's website (https://riverfrontnorth.org).

EQUIPMENT: Comfortable shoes are all you'll need on this flat, level trail. A magnifying glass might help as you study the finer details of slime molds.

GUIDED VIEWING: Although I have never encountered a slime mold–focused walk, Riverfront North offers plenty of general nature walks at Pennypack on the Delaware and along the Baxter Trail. Fungus-themed walks—for example, with the Philadelphia Mycology Club—at any location are also great opportunities to find slime molds.

OTHER LOCATIONS: Slime molds are not limited to parks, and indeed you can find them in your garden or other places with soil and dead vegetation.

KIDS: Slime molds are harmless and have names that kids can't help but find compelling. What child could resist looking for "wolf's milk" or getting permission to gag over "dog vomit," all while learning about soil ecology?

III. Summer

27

Bats, Balls, and Birds
Spot Nighthawks at the Ballpark

EVEN BASEBALL FANS WILL ADMIT that there's plenty of time to watch birds during a game. You don't have to keep your eyes on the field every time the sides change or the manager sends in yet another relief pitcher. Why not look up at the birds flying around the stadium?

The usual neighborhood birds will be there, such as pigeons, starlings, sparrows, and crows. You might spot an eastern kingbird perched on a wire near the field. Chimney swifts and swallows might catch bugs as they fly. And as the sun sets and the diurnal birds settle down to sleep, nighthawks take to the air. Not really hawks, these long-winged birds, a little smaller than pigeons, fly at dusk and dawn, using their wide mouths to snap up flying insects. Many of those flying insects are attracted to the stadium lights, and the nighthawks go where the bugs are.

Outside the city, nighthawks nest on bare ground. In the city, flat gravel roofs suit them just fine, making them relatively common in urban Philadelphia.

As the sun starts to set, look up. You'll see moths, caddisflies, and other insects, looking a bit like snow swirling in the stadium lights. Stay alert for birds with relatively long wings flying about. Nighthawks sport white patches toward the ends of their long wings, which can help distinguish them from the pigeons and other birds attending the game. They don't show up every night, but neither do the Phillies' bats. Thankfully, Philly baseball fans and birders alike know how to forget disappointment.

Beyond the stadium, you can find nighthawks taking advantage of lights at local parks' playing fields. They also hunt above fields and cemeteries, and you can sometimes hear them above the blocks where they nest and hunt. Nighthawks call with a buzzy "peent." In the breeding season, males add in a "boom" effect created by their wings as they dive.

WHERE: Citizens Bank Park

ACCESS: You have to buy tickets to go to Phillies games, so consider the birding a free bonus. Citizens Bank Park is accessible from the Broad Street subway line.

WHEN: Nighthawks arrive from South America in early May and stay through most of the baseball season, departing in September and October.

EQUIPMENT: You can see the nighthawks with the naked eye, but binoculars will help you make out the details. Peanuts, Cracker Jack, and ice cream in little batting helmets are all optional.

GUIDED VIEWING: Although bat walks (at places like the Woodlands cemetery or Pennypack on the Delaware) focus on flying mammals, the timing is great for seeing nighthawks as well. These dusk-flying birds usually show up a little before the bats do, often tricking eager bat watchers. Once you know what to look for, you'll be ready on your next trip to the ballpark.

OTHER LOCATIONS: Search open grassy areas, such as cemeteries and playing fields at dusk, and learn to listen for the birds' "peent" call wherever you are.

KIDS: If your child is old enough to go to a night game, they are old enough to spot birds while they're there.

28

Drop a Line
Go Fishing

I WAS PADDLING ON THE LOWER SCHUYLKILL when I saw a channel catfish slowly lifting up into the air. A man fishing from a park on the east bank pulled it in. It was the only fish I saw in my morning out on the water. Whether we are paddling or walking along the bank, we might be lucky to see a fish jump or dart away as a dark shape under the surface. Fishing gives us a closer look. Sure, anyone might think of fishing in some picturesque mountain stream or off the beach at the Jersey Shore, but our urban waterways are also worth casting into. By doing so, you can learn exactly how alive they really are.

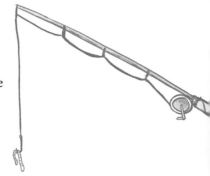

If you have never fished before and aren't sure how to tell a rod from a reel, take advantage of an introductory fishing program. Riverfront North, for example, offers fishing instruction, complete with bait and equipment, at multiple sites along the Delaware River waterfront in Northeast Philadelphia. Instructors are on hand to guide you through the basics and help you catch the fish you're looking for.

You could also do worse than buying a very cheap rod and reel (or excavating the one you've got out of the back of the garage), digging up a worm, and casting into whatever body of water is near you.

Small, feisty fish like red-breasted sunfish and bluegill abound in our ponds and smaller creeks. They might not impress your neighbors as a trophy on the wall, but they'll give you a lot of fun.

Consider bringing along a temporary holding tank (a large jar, fish tank, or acrylic box) and filling it with water when you get to where you're fishing. A fish flopping about on the end of a line looks less impressive than it does in its element. After taking a minute to admire the fish, let it go and repeat.

WHERE: Riverfront North offers fishing programs at Pleasant Hill Park, the Frankford Boat Launch, and Pulaski Park.

ACCESS: The fishing piers along the Delaware River can be reached by car or by SEPTA.

WHEN: July and August

FOR MORE INFORMATION: Visit Riverfront North's website (https://riverfrontnorth.org/) for up-to-date information on its fishing program. Visit the Pennsylvania Fish and Boat Commission's website (https://www.fishandboat.com/Fish/FishingFundamentals) for more information on getting started in fishing.

Also, check out Leo Sheng's Extreme Philly Fishing channels on YouTube and other social media. Sheng, who shares his exploits through his YouTube channel and other social media, practices multispecies fishing. The goal is not just to have fun hooking a fish or taking home dinner but to explore the biodiversity of a waterway through fishing.

EQUIPMENT: Introductory fishing programs generally supply equipment. You might also need a fishing license (which you'll always need when fishing independently), so check before you get started.

OTHER LOCATIONS: Other parks and organizations offer fishing programming, including the John Heinz National Wildlife Refuge at Tinicum, where you can borrow equipment at the visitor center.

KIDS: These programs are well suited to fishing with children. While grown-ups might be disappointed by smaller fish, children are usually thrilled to catch anything, and releasing the fish is its own special event.

29

Go with the Current
Paddle an Urban River

I HAD NEVER CONSIDERED whether an alligator snapping turtle, a creature of Southern waterways, could thrive in Philadelphia until I found one on a paddling trip on the tidal Schuylkill River. Neither had I considered how many grackles and kingbirds forage along the shorelines until I paddled on the Delaware. And I had never suspected that rats would join them, emerging at low tide to check the shorelines of eroded brick and stone fill (old buildings dumped to extend the land) for food left high and dry by the receding water.

Rivers are not just obstacles to cross over, and we get a new perspective on nature by viewing them from the water's surface: watching fish jump, beaver harvest vegetation to eat, or swallows catch insects out of the air and skim the surface, dipping just close enough to get a drink and then pull up. Paddling lets us experience aquatic ecosystems more intimately than we ever could from a bridge or even a trail along the bank.

Getting out on the water can take a little work, unfortunately. Although anyone can go to a boat launch and push off, boating presents very real hazards. All watersports present the risk of drowning, and our tidal rivers add the challenge of strong currents that switch directions. We also share the water with much larger boats, from pleasure craft up to freighters. All of this means that beginners should be cautious and start out under expert supervision.

The Center for Aquatic Sciences at Adventure Aquarium offers family kayak tours at Pyne Poynt Park in

Camden, New Jersey, where the Cooper River meets the Delaware. The back channel on the New Jersey side of Petty's Island there offers sheltered paddling, and the guides will help point out plants and animals of interest as you go. As you learn how to safely navigate our urban waters and, perhaps, invest in watercraft, you can venture out on your own.

Much of the wildlife you share the water with will steer clear of you, just as on land. The long, clear lines of sight that make boating so scenic mean that turtles, birds, and other critters will, in turn, see you and either take off or dive. Bringing binoculars will make it much easier to watch them from a comfortable distance. Also, pay attention to the angle of the sun. Whether birds or turtles, backlighting makes everything look like little silhouettes with no detail, so keep the sun at your back whenever possible.

WHERE: Pyne Poynt Park in Camden, New Jersey

ACCESS: Pyne Poynt Park is easy to reach by car.

WHEN: The Center for Aquatic Sciences at Adventure Aquarium offers kayaking programs during warmer months of the year.

FOR MORE INFORMATION: Check the center's website (https://www.aquaticsciences.org/) for the calendar of kayaking events and other important information.

EQUIPMENT: Dress to get wet and avoid bringing anything that you need to keep dry. Binoculars will help you observe wildlife.

OTHER LOCATIONS: Several waterfront organizations offer programs to get you on the water, including Schuylkill Banks, the Independence Seaport Museum, and Bartram's Garden.

KIDS: This is suitable for older children who can handle paddles. The Center for Aquatic Sciences at Adventure Aquarium requires paddlers to be at least eight years old.

30

Nature's Fireworks
Watch Fireflies

I TOOK MY DAUGHTER MAGNOLIA, then five years old, to a summer firefly event, where we did arts and crafts and waited for it to get dark enough for the fireflies to start their phosphorescent dance above the grass. I am a stickler for punctual bedtimes. As it got darker so very slowly, I imagined the consequences of a cranky, sleep-deprived child the next morning. Finally, a couple of fireflies lit up. It was a little like visual whack-a-mole at first because by the time I could point one out, that flash had dimmed, but finally she saw a couple on her own. I felt safe to load her in the bike trailer and ride home. As we rode past the tiny but lush front gardens of the Spruce Hill neighborhood of West Philadelphia, Magnolia spoke up. "There's one," she said, "and there's one."

Fireflies (aka lightning bugs) are beetles that use light-emitting organs in their abdomens to communicate back and forth during their summer mating season, essentially finding each other in the dark. Females of some species even imitate the flashing patterns of others so they can eat the males they lure in.

While fireflies evoke muggy evenings in the country (big porches, lemonade, rocking chairs), you can also find fireflies flashing over small patches of green in the city. Our

backyard is flagstone with three raised beds, for a total of thirty-six square feet of greenery, and we have fireflies in the summer.

That said, nothing beats seeing hundreds of fireflies light up open spaces like cemeteries or meadows, mirroring the stars above. It feels truly magical, and one could be excused for imagining fairies at work instead of beetles looking for love.

And if by the Fourth of July you are tired of the artificial light and sternum-rattling booms of fireworks, you can celebrate the peak of summer by finding a nice open space to watch as fireflies put on a more peaceful but fully dazzling show. The Wissahickon Environmental Center (aka the "Tree House") offers Firefly Fireworks programs at Andorra Meadow at the edge of the Wissahickon Valley in Northwest Philadelphia.

WHERE: Andorra Meadow is at the edge of the Wissahickon Valley along Northwestern Avenue in Philadelphia.

ACCESS: Andorra Meadow is easy to reach from the Andorra Upper Lot parking lot on Northwestern Avenue. It is a ten-minute walk from the bus stop at Ridge Avenue. The trail surfaces are natural.

WHEN: Fireflies light up the night during the middle of the summer, and firefly walks and events tend to be held in June and July.

FOR MORE INFORMATION: You can find event information on the Wissahickon Environmental Center Facebook Page (https://www.facebook.com/TreeHouseWEC).

OTHER LOCATIONS: Generally, urban parks are closed after dark, but many parks, nature centers, and other green spaces, such as the Woodlands cemetery, hold firefly events, so check their summer calendars for a firefly night near you.

KIDS: Any child will enjoy the lights of fireflies at night. It's fun to catch them temporarily in clear jars to watch them light up, and the phosphorescence can be sweetly disarming, so that kids who are usually grossed out by bugs will catch a firefly and watch it glow in their hand.

31

Fun Guys
Go on a Mushroom Hunt

A FRIEND AND I WERE SEARCHING for snakes at an overgrown, postindustrial site in Northeast Philadelphia when I noticed something odd growing out of the thin, dusty soil: little cones with a netlike surface.

I had eaten morels several times in my life, and they are absolutely delicious. I knew that people hunted for morels out in the woods. I didn't think of this abandoned industrial site as forest, exactly, but looking around, I realized that twenty years or so of neglect had indeed yielded a stand of trees where we were standing, apparently enough for the fungus to develop through their roots in the ground beneath our feet.

In a way, we do a disservice to fungi by focusing so much on their value to our taste buds. Fungi, living out of sight as networks of threadlike structures called "hyphae," play incredibly important ecological roles. For example, they break down dead plant matter, and several species live in symbiosis with plants by growing into their roots and helping them take up soil nutrients (morel species can fall into either category). You can observe fungi without finding mushrooms. When you turn over a log in a forest and find it almost knitted to the ground with densely packed white threads, you're looking at hyphae.

These masses of hyphae can spend years growing where we can't see them, only to reproduce when the moment is right. Mushrooms are the fruiting bodies, the structures fungi use to disperse their spores.

Search for mushrooms by heading for the nearest woods and studying all the surfaces you can find. Mushrooms pop out of the ground, of course, but you can find species that parasitize trees growing out of bark, and, of course, varieties that break down dead wood will be sprouting out of logs. Timing and moisture matter because fungi often grow their fruiting bodies in response to rain.

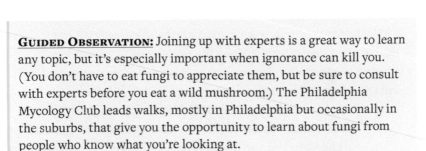

GUIDED OBSERVATION: Joining up with experts is a great way to learn any topic, but it's especially important when ignorance can kill you. (You don't have to eat fungi to appreciate them, but be sure to consult with experts before you eat a wild mushroom.) The Philadelphia Mycology Club leads walks, mostly in Philadelphia but occasionally in the suburbs, that give you the opportunity to learn about fungi from people who know what you're looking at.

WHEN: The Philadelphia Mycology Club holds walks in the spring through the fall. In the dead of winter, you can still take part in mushroom-themed craft events.

FOR MORE INFORMATION: Follow the Philadelphia Mycology Club on Facebook (https://www.facebook.com/phillymycoclub), on Instagram (@PhillyMycoClub), or by email (philamycologyclub@gmail.com).

EQUIPMENT: Comfortable shoes for hiking are all you need, but a magnifying glass or loupe can help you make out some of the finer details.

OTHER LOCATIONS: Mushroom walks are popular programs at many nature centers and parks, so keep an eye on local activity calendars for a walk near you.

KIDS: This is an activity that requires no special equipment and is well suited for kids old enough to go on a walk.

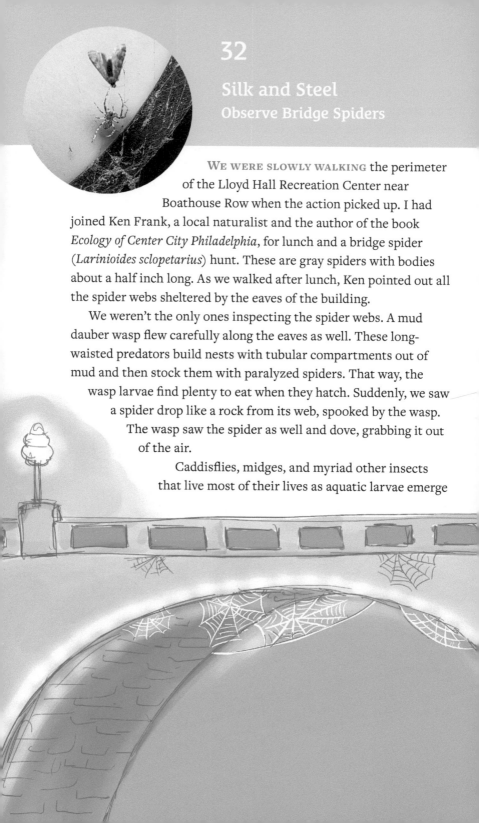

32

Silk and Steel
Observe Bridge Spiders

WE WERE SLOWLY WALKING the perimeter of the Lloyd Hall Recreation Center near Boathouse Row when the action picked up. I had joined Ken Frank, a local naturalist and the author of the book *Ecology of Center City Philadelphia*, for lunch and a bridge spider (*Larinioides sclopetarius*) hunt. These are gray spiders with bodies about a half inch long. As we walked after lunch, Ken pointed out all the spider webs sheltered by the eaves of the building.

We weren't the only ones inspecting the spider webs. A mud dauber wasp flew carefully along the eaves as well. These long-waisted predators build nests with tubular compartments out of mud and then stock them with paralyzed spiders. That way, the wasp larvae find plenty to eat when they hatch. Suddenly, we saw a spider drop like a rock from its web, spooked by the wasp. The wasp saw the spider as well and dove, grabbing it out of the air.

Caddisflies, midges, and myriad other insects that live most of their lives as aquatic larvae emerge for a brief adult phase to mate and lay eggs. They join moths and other terrestrial insects that fly at night. Spiders that spin their webs on structures near the water end up in a great position to catch all of these flying insects. Bridge spiders are particularly attracted to artificial light, and you can also often find their webs around streetlamps. While you can find the webs any time, the spiders are easy to observe in hunting position in the evening, when you can also see their prey flying around lights. On a bridge or lamppost with lots of webs, you can see a lucky spider rush over to a struggling (and profoundly unlucky) insect, wrap it with silk, and dig in.

While you're searching for bridge spiders, keep an eye out for the nests of the mud daubers in the same places. You might be able to see wasps coming in and out, sometimes bearing paralyzed spiders.

WHERE: The Lloyd Hall Recreation Center is on the east bank of the Schuylkill River in Philadelphia, near Boathouse Row and the Fairmount Water Works.

ACCESS: The paved Schuylkill River Trail, which goes past the center, is open day and night and easily reached by the 38 bus stop at the Philadelphia Museum of Art.

WHEN: Summer is a good time to observe the spiders.

FOR MORE INFORMATION: Ken Frank's book *Ecology of Center City Philadelphia* has a chapter on bridge spiders. You can read it online (http://fitlersquarepress.com/ecology-of-center-city-philadelphia/).

EQUIPMENT: The spiders are easy to observe with the naked eye, but binoculars might help you take a closer look.

OTHER LOCATIONS: Look for bridge spiders on bridges and other structures.

KIDS: Checking out spider webs is easy for kids of any age, but older kids with later bedtimes might have an easier time observing spider activity.

33

A Flap in the Night
Go on a Bat Walk

Was that a bat? I always doubt the first
bat I see. I'm used to watching birds, and this is
no different in a cemetery or any other bat-viewing
spot. Swallows zip between the trees and through the clearings,
picking bugs out of the air. Chimney swifts skim over the treetops.
Nighthawks might show up to
join the feast at dusk.
After all the birds,
my brain works
hard to trust the
first bat in the
dimming light as it
just catches my eye
and then disappears
around a tree. In a minute
or two, more bats help
confirm the first as the birds cede the
air to them.

Our bat populations, particularly the
previously common little brown bats, took
a huge hit from white-nose syndrome. This fungal
infection interrupts hibernation, causing bats to burn
through winter fat reserves prematurely and starve to
death. Other species can still be found, including big brown bats,
which I've seen flying over my own West Philly rooftop, as well as
hoary, eastern red, and silver-haired bats. All of our bats hide out
during the day. At night, they gobble up flying insects, navigating by
echolocation.

We tend not to notice bats due to the hours they keep. We
sleep while they are flying, and parks tend to be closed after dark.
Bat nights give us the chance to observe bats in action. At the

Woodlands, a historic cemetery in West Philadelphia, for example, experts lead walks and point out the bats taking to the air at dusk. The more you get to know bats, the less spooky they will seem, but there is still something magical about watching bats fly above a cemetery as night falls.

Some bat nights feature bat detectors—devices set to monitor the audio frequencies bats use to navigate and that can distinguish bat species by the differences in the sounds they produce.

WHERE: The Woodlands entrance is on Woodland Avenue in West Philadelphia, just across the street from the 40th Street Trolley Portal.

ACCESS: The cemetery is open from dusk to dawn. To come late enough to see the bats, attend their annual bat night or other Nature Nights events, such as moth and firefly nights. The cemetery is easy to reach by SEPTA. There are paved paths throughout the grounds.

WHEN: The Woodlands Nature Nights series runs monthly through the summer, and it offers other nature walks during the day through the year.

FOR MORE INFORMATION: Get in touch with the Woodlands (https://www.woodlandsphila.org) to see its calendar and learn about upcoming nature events.

EQUIPMENT: Comfortable walking shoes are all you'll need for the paved, brick, and grass paths through the cemetery. You can buy your own bat detector if you'd like to monitor bats after it gets too dark to see them and identify them down to the species.

OTHER LOCATIONS: Many local nature centers, parks, and cemeteries offer guided night walks to observe bats and other nocturnal animals. It's also worth staking out your backyard or roof at dusk to try to spot them closer to home.

KIDS: Bat nights, like most environmental education events at parks, welcome families with children. The hard part of observing bats with children is how late you have to keep them up, especially in the summer. Luckily, bats fly into early fall, when the sun sets a little earlier.

34

Zombie Patrol
Find a Dead Zombie Fly

EVERY YEAR, I'M SLIGHTLY DISAPPOINTED by all the green bottle flies that hang out around the flowers blooming in the containers in front of our house. They are particularly fond of the swamp milkweed and brown-eyed Susans that peak in July. Of course, the shiny green flies are actually kind of pretty when you get past their life history (developing from the pale, wriggling maggots feeding on scraps of meat in the trash), but I feel a slight bit of satisfaction to see them dead and stuck to the ends of leaves of the same plants whose flowers they adore.

What kills them and sticks them to the end of the leaves is a fungus called *Entomophthora muscae*. Its spores land on a fly, and its hyphae (the threadlike structures that make up most of a fungus) grow into the victim, eventually reaching its brain and taking it over. There, they guide the fly to land high up on a plant at the tip of a leaf, stretch out its wings, and touch the leaf with its proboscis, which is then attached to the leaf. This holds the fly in place once it dies. There, the fungus's spores will rain down onto other unlucky flies. In the cruelest twist of all, male flies will sometimes try to mate with fungus-killed females, picking up spores and spreading them to live females they mate with later.

Keep an eye out for flies sitting on the undersides of leaf tips, particularly high up on a plant. You'll have the best luck with plants near where you see lots of flies—for example, near your trash cans.

Go ahead and see whether you can give the fly a poke. A live fly will escape, but these dead flies will stay stuck to the leaf.

Take a good look at the fly's abdomen. The fungus grows through the segments of its exoskeleton, visible as an off-white substance that seems to be welling up and expanding out of the gaps. That's where the fungus produces the spores that will reach the next flies and digest them from the inside as they hijack their brains.

Flies are hardly the only insect that falls victim to pathogenic fungi. Other fungi do pretty much the same thing to moths, cicadas, and ants, eating them from the inside and taking over their brains as part of their final reproductive strategy. Keep an eye out for dead bugs in oddly high places and take a closer look when you find them. (Note: All of these insect-killing fungi are harmless to humans.)

WHERE: Anywhere you find flies and plants

WHEN: Spring through fall

EQUIPMENT: A magnifying glass will help you study the detail of the fungus and its fly victim.

KIDS: What could be cooler than a fungus that turns flies into zombies and eats them from the inside?

35

Pollinator Party!
Visit a Milkweed Patch

EXITING THE WOODS and walking up to the blooming milkweed patch at the Hildacy Preserve feels a little bit like opening the door to an apartment and stumbling into a raging party. Butterflies and bees bump around and knock each other out of the way in a competition for what a watching human can only conclude must be the best nectar in the world. Large and small milkweed bugs (true bugs, with an orange and black warning pattern common to the critters that feed on milkweed and end up retaining some of the plant's toxins as a defense against predators) suck the plants' juices straight from the stems and seed pods. Red milkweed beetles feed and mate in the open, and smaller bees and flies hover about and dart in to feed.

Milkweed gets a lot of attention for being the host plant for monarch butterflies. The continent's most famous butterfly is in decline. This has focused attention on the genuinely weedy common milkweed, which springs up in patches in vacant lots, power line cuts, and meadows.

Look for the black, yellow, and white-banded monarch caterpillars eating the leaves of the milkweed, but don't stop there. It is also easy to spot other black-and-orange critters that feed on milkweed, and a milkweed patch is a great place to observe a wide

WHERE: The meadow at the Hildacy Preserve in Delaware County features a large patch of milkweed in Hilda's Meadow, just a few minutes' walk from the parking lot on the red, green, or yellow hiking trails.

ACCESS: Hildacy can be reached by car and charges no admission. The paths are natural surface.

WHEN: Milkweed blooms from mid-June into July.

FOR MORE INFORMATION: Visit the Natural Lands' Hildacy Preserve's website (https://natlands.org/hildacypreserve/).

EQUIPMENT: This is a light hike, so sneakers or other shoes suitable for a walk on dirt or grass trails will do. Most of the insect action is visible to the naked eye, but a magnifying glass can help reveal more detail, and binoculars can help you observe skittish butterflies.

GUIDED VIEWING: Check the Natural Lands' website (https://natlands.org) for a schedule of walks and other events at Hildacy.

OTHER LOCATIONS: Milkweed is easy to find growing in unmowed, sunny settings.

KIDS: Milkweed makes entomology easy. Kids can see brightly colored bugs, big and bold butterflies, and swarms of bees and other pollinators.

variety of non–monarch butterflies coming to drink nectar. Keep an eye out for fuzzy caterpillars as well. Just like the monarch butterfly, the milkweed tussock moth sequesters the milkweed's toxins. As a nocturnal animal, though, the plain gray moth warns predatory bats through sound, not colors.

36

The Jewels of Summer
Meet the Butterflies

AS MUCH AS I DO ADMIRE all the bees and other pollinators (even the flies!), butterflies remain in a separate class. When a great spangled fritillary flutters in like a glowing swatch of the sunset, it's hard to look at anything else. The same is true from the equally dramatic swallowtails on down to the postage stamp–sized tailed blues.

A midsummer trip to Tyler Arboretum turned up butterflies throughout the grounds, feeding on such flowers as the vivid magenta blooms of the New York ironweed. At the butterfly house, we watched an assortment of swallowtails and a monarch and got to see a monarch caterpillar, banded in white, black, yellow, and green, hiding under a milkweed leaf.

You can get to know your local butterflies in many ways. You can plant native flowering plants and watch what comes in to visit, for example, and you can keep an eye on pollinator hotspots, such as flowering trees, milkweed patches, and meadows. Your local environmental center likely offers butterfly-focused walks and programs in the summer.

Native butterfly houses offer a concentrated dose of butterfly exposure and learning, with the insects easy to spot. Essentially, they are greenhouses growing native plants—species that host caterpillars as well as those whose flowers feed adults.

The support from volunteers and signage make it easy to figure out what is what. Later, you'll see the same species flying wherever else you go and recognize them. Perhaps just as important, establishing familiarity with a few common species helps you figure out identification when you're looking at something else (orange and black, kind of like a fritillary, but with a band of white spots—Baltimore checkerspot?).

WHERE: Tyler Arboretum is in Delaware County.

ACCESS: The arboretum is best reached by car. It is open during the day and charges admission, so check the website for details about hours and costs. The paths through the core of the arboretum are mostly paved, and the butterfly-house paths are gravel.

WHEN: The butterfly house is generally open in July and August.

FOR MORE INFORMATION: Visit the arboretum's website (https://tylerarboretum.org).

EQUIPMENT: You should be able to observe the butterflies with the naked eye, but a pair of binoculars can help you observe skittish butterflies in more detail.

GUIDED VIEWING: The butterfly house is staffed by volunteers who can help you find and learn more about the butterflies at all life stages. Tyler also offers butterfly walks led by docents.

OTHER LOCATIONS: The Churchville Nature Center in lower Bucks County also has a butterfly house with a full menu of other butterfly activities, including tagging monarch butterflies before their migration.

KIDS: This is a great way for kids to get to know butterflies and is well suited for all ages.

37

What They Do in the Dark
Hold a Moth Night

EVERYONE LOVES BUTTERFLIES. They flutter along as we ooh and ahh at their bright colors—the yellow of the sulfurs, the orange of the fritillaries, the scarlet of the red admirals, or the velvety blue of the pipevine swallowtails. We plant our gardens to give them somewhere to feed, and museums build climate-controlled butterfly rooms so visitors can get a closer look.

No one builds a moth room, but perhaps they should. Butterflies are far outnumbered by their earth-toned relatives that take the stage after dark. Pennsylvania hosts about 160 species of butterflies, but we have more than two thousand types of moth. Moths can be more challenging to tell apart than butterflies, with subtle patterns that help them blend in rather than stand out. Nonetheless, you can get a taste for their diversity by staying up a little later and attending a moth night event.

A moth night is a great way to get introduced to the world of night-flying insects. Experts lure in the moths with lights placed conveniently close to white sheets that give the moths a surface to land on and be observed. They might also paint trees with bait (some mix of fruit, sugar, and alcohol) that attract moths looking for an easy meal. With enough people who know what

they're doing, along with the right guidebooks, visitors can start to learn how to tell the different species apart.

Bartram's Garden hosts just such an event, taking advantage of its mix of meadow and forest habitat as well as the darkness offered by its extensive grounds away from buildings or streetlights.

WHERE: Bartram's Garden is located in Southwest Philadelphia, just off Lindbergh Boulevard.

ACCESS: Moth nights generally occur after regular hours, so check the events calendar. Some paths are paved, but others, particularly in the darker corners where the moth night activities are focused, are natural surfaces. Bartram's Garden is easily reached by car or by SEPTA.

WHEN: Moth nights are generally scheduled during the summer, but you can observe moths flying into the fall.

FOR MORE INFORMATION: Visit Bartram's Garden's website (https://www.bartramsgarden.org/) to check the events calendar and learn more about the garden.

EQUIPMENT: Moth nights at Bartram's Garden and other venues provide all the necessary equipment. If you're observing moths on your own, any source of light, whether a flashlight or a porchlight, will draw them in. Try a blacklight bulb for a more powerful lure. Hanging a white sheet in the glow of the light gives the critters a place to land where you can get a good look at them.

OTHER LOCATIONS: Many nature centers and parks in the area offer moth nights, so check the summer schedules wherever you enjoy green space. Also, you are probably already hosting moth nights without even realizing it. Every time you leave the porch light on after dark from spring through fall, you have the opportunity to observe the moths and other nocturnal critters drawn in by the glow.

KIDS: Moth nights, whether a public event or at your own home, are huge hits with kids. The only obstacle is the timing because the action picks up after dark. Luckily, moths fly into late summer and early autumn, when staying up past sunset might be a little easier.

38

Swoop into Summer
Watch Chimney Swifts

IN LATE APRIL, an excited twittering sound drifts down from above the rooftops. It's the first time I've heard it for about six months, and I search the sky above for the chimney swifts, just returned from their winter in South America. Finally, I see the birds, with cigar-shaped bodies and curved wings held stiffly like a drawn bow. They fly in long glides powered by bursts of rapid, fluttering strokes as they pick bugs out of the air.

Chimney swifts once nested and roosted primarily inside large hollow trees. As European colonists replaced old forests with brick and stone buildings, the birds shifted to nesting on the interiors of chimneys and other structures. The birds are so devoted to life on the wing that their tiny legs are useless for walking or even standing on flat ground—all they can do is cling to vertical surfaces. Luckily for the swifts, our cities have lots of old chimneys to nest and roost inside and plenty of flying insects overhead.

Keep an eye out for swifts overhead, but also pay attention to their twittering calls, often the first clue that they're there. You might confuse swifts with swallows, which also fly around catching bugs out of the air, but pay attention to how they fly. Swifts tend to flutter rapidly (a little like bats) and then glide in relatively long arcs higher in the air, while swallows use deeper wing beats and display much more agility, zipping and dodging, often quite close to the ground or the surface of a body of water. Swifts, like most animals, tend to avoid the hottest times of

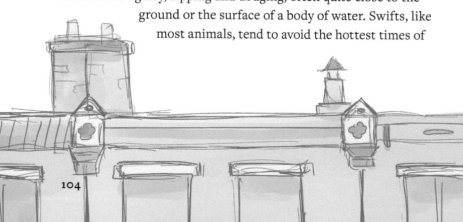

sunny summer days, so look for them in the morning, in the early evening before sunset, and as humid winds pick up before a storm.

While swifts are easy to spot on the wing, a little sleuthing can reveal where they finally alight. Nesting swifts will return to the chimney or other structure where they have used their saliva to glue their nests to the wall to incubate eggs or feed chicks. You can spot the returning swift abruptly stop its glide and, in an awkward move, pitch itself down into the opening. In the fall, you can spot larger flocks of swifts roosting together for the night in larger structures, such as smokestacks or school chimneys. Hundreds of the birds will swirl around in a tighter and tighter vortex, finally flying into the opening like a cloud of smoke in reverse.

WHERE: Chimney swifts fly throughout the region.

ACCESS: Chimney swifts can be observed from nearly any sidewalk with a view of the sky.

WHEN: Chimney swifts show up in April and leave again in October or early November.

EQUIPMENT: Binoculars can help reveal more detail, but swifts are easy to observe with the naked eye.

GUIDED VIEWING: Join an urban or neighborhood birding walk, such as those held by BirdPhilly (https://birdphilly.org), to have expert birders point swifts out to you.

KIDS: Swifts are easy to spot and follow, and finding their nests can be a fun nature detective project.

39

Wildflower Preserves
Press Flowers

WE HAVE BEEN WORKING ON an art project for the house, pressing flowers from our garden. The plan is to frame and display them on our walls. The larger, showier flowers that we intentionally grow are obvious choices, but I lobbied to include some of the "weeds" as well because the unintentional plants (such as the humble copperleaf mercury or the irrepressible white snakeroot) are part of the plant community as well, even if I rarely let them grow to maturity.

Pressing flowers is nothing new. Artists have incorporated pressed flowers into artwork for centuries (for example, Oshibana in Japan), and, of course, a museum herbarium is a scientific collection composed of carefully pressed plants.

Pressing plants is a great way to step into botany. For starters, it gives you the opportunity to look at plant features that distinguish one type from another. Are the stems fuzzy or smooth? How do the leaves attach to the stem—with little stalks (petioles) or by wrapping around (clasping)? As you compare your samples, you can get the hang of identifying plants, a skill that will serve you in the field. Beyond that, gathering plants while they're flowering can tune you in to their "phenology" or individual timing through the seasons.

You can build your own herbarium with dried plants, or you can press flowers for art projects. For example, you can attach them to greeting cards, or you can end up mounting them on the wall as a more enduring decoration.

Pressing plants can be as simple as placing them between the pages of a book. Indeed, I was recently reading through a particularly large plant guide when a dried flower dropped out. I apparently had previously been identifying the plant and had absentmindedly closed the book on it.

You'll get the best results with a few easy steps to ensure quick drying. First, start with fresh specimens. You want to preserve them before they start wilting. The goal is then to dry them out while weighting them to preserve their shape. Fold the plant into a sheet of newspaper and then layer it on either side with corrugated cardboard. You can keep stacking more plant samples and cardboard, creating a multilayer sandwich of cardboard, paper, and plants.

Museums use plant presses consisting of wooden frames on the top and bottom with straps to keep the whole stack together. You can do something similar with whatever scrap wood you've got in the basement plus some weights or particularly heavy books. The goal is to keep the stack under even pressure without individual layers sliding out. Wait about ten days or do what we do and forget about them for a few weeks until you encounter the pile of books in the corner of the room and remember what they're doing there.

WHERE: Collect plants in your garden, sidewalk, vacant lots, or other places where picking them is permitted (when in doubt, ask) and then press them at home.

FOR MORE INFORMATION: There are many guides to pressing plants online, and local nature centers and arboretums often offer classes on artwork incorporating pressed flowers and other plant parts.

EQUIPMENT: You can do a lot with newspaper, cardboard, and some coffee-table books. You could also buy a plant press or build one out of wood and straps. You can mount pressed plants to paper with white craft glue.

KIDS: This is an easy and accessible activity for any child who likes arts and crafts. You can tailor the sophistication of the project to the abilities of the child.

IV. Autumn

40

Messing with Squirrels Has Never Been More Fun
Go Squirrel Fishing

I LOCKED EYES WITH THE SQUIRREL, something that I wasn't expecting when I tossed the peanut out on the end of my line toward my bushy-tailed quarry. I had assumed the squirrels would view the peanut as an object independent of the human standing eight or so feet away. Surely, the monofilament line connecting me, via rod and reel, to the peanut would be all but invisible as the squirrel focused on the tasty treat at the end of it. I was wrong. This one seemed to understand immediately that I was responsible for this peanut that somehow fought back, resisting the pull of its paws as it tried to retrieve it to chew through the shell and eat the kernels at a safer distance.

I got the critter off the ground—the goal of squirrel fishing— dangling by its front paws for a second before it chewed a hole in the shell, got its prize, and let go. I did not manage to suspend that squirrel again, however. The second time, it upped its own game by immediately biting through the fishing line and running away with the peanut.

Squirrel fishing sounds wackier than it actually is, but maybe only by a little. This is similar to fishing for fish. The key difference is that instead of tying your line to a hook or a lure, you tie it around an unshelled peanut. You then toss the peanut out to a squirrel and wait for it to pick up the bait. When it does, you start reeling it in and lifting. The squirrel can release the bait at any time, and your goal is to get the squirrel off the ground before it lets go or frees the nut.

Be sure to choose a place where squirrels are already used to getting food from humans and start by tossing out a few untied peanuts to get them in the feeding mood.

CAVEAT: Wildlife feeding bans are generally selectively enforced. In other words, plenty of people don't get in trouble for feeding birds or squirrels. Parks near you might have more restrictive rules and tighter enforcement depending on the local circumstances, however.

WHEN: You can squirrel fish at any time of year, but this is a great activity for fall and winter months, when you can enjoy a crisp day on a park bench.

FOR MORE INFORMATION: The Internet and social media are full of interactive squirrel-feeding examples. These include squirrel obstacle courses as well as squirrel-powered kinetic sculptures.

EQUIPMENT: You need a fishing rod and reel as well as fishing line. Err on the side of a stiffer rod and heavier-test line. Squirrels don't weigh more than a couple of pounds, but you are fighting them entirely in the air.

KIDS: Any child old enough to handle a fishing rod should enjoy this.

41

Glorious Gobblers
Find Wild Turkeys

WE HAD JUST PARKED at the Cramer Hill Nature Preserve in Camden, New Jersey, and were sorting through the sundry tasks of a family nature walk (Sunblock? Binoculars? Need help putting on the baby carrier?) when a turkey leisurely strolled across the street from the surrounding neighborhood and into the preserve. The glossy black, svelte bird didn't look much like the white, overstuffed domestic turkey doomed to anchor Thanksgiving dinners. Separated by five hundred or so years of domestication, the wild bird looked more leggy and elegant. It made no noise, and I would have missed it if I hadn't happened to be facing in its direction.

Wild turkeys always surprise me. They are large birds, but they move quietly and seem to come out of nowhere, no matter how many times I see them. The same is true for urbanites throughout their range, most of whom don't expect to see a large wild bird walking around like it owns the neighborhood. After centuries of overhunting, government protection and restocking efforts by state game agencies starting in the 1950s have proven to be so successful[1] that the birds have expanded their range into cities from Pittsburgh to Boston.

Searching for turkeys is simply a matter of walking around where they live and keeping your eyes peeled. Be sure to study muddy sections of trail for their large footprints: three big toes forward, one small toe back. Turkeys form flocks in the fall, so as soon as you spot

---

1. National Wild Turkey Federation, "Wild Turkey Population History and Overview," accessed October 29, 2020, https://www.nwtf.org/_resources/dyn/files/75706989za3010574/_fn/Wild+Turkey+Population+History+and+Overview.pdf.

one on a nature walk at that time of year, get the stragglers in your own group up to the front and watch quietly to see the rest of the birds strut across your path.

Although they can be seen foraging year-round, late winter is breeding season, and you can find the toms strutting about with their chests puffed up and magnificent tails fanned out, like something straight out of a Thanksgiving Day parade. While in other seasons turkeys will scoot out of view once they see humans, breeding toms are less timid and can put on a show. They also sometimes mistake their reflections in cars for rival birds and go on the attack.

WHERE: The Cramer Hill Nature Preserve is in Camden, New Jersey, along the bank of the Delaware River across from Petty's Island.

ACCESS: The preserve is easy to reach by car and offers parking off 36th Street in Camden. The trails are natural surface.

WHEN: Turkeys can be seen year-round.

FOR MORE INFORMATION: Check out Camden County's website for the preserve (http://www.ccmua.org/index.php/cramer-hill-nature -preserve/) as well as the Virtually Camden resources at the Center for Aquatic Sciences at Adventure Aquarium (https://www.aquaticsciences .org/community/Trails.html).

EQUIPMENT: Wear comfortable walking shoes. Turkeys are easy to spot with the naked eye, so you shouldn't need binoculars.

OTHER LOCATIONS: Turkeys can be seen at other parks along the Delaware River in South Jersey as well as in Pennsylvania in Southwest Philadelphia (e.g., the John Heinz National Wildlife Refuge at Tinicum and Bartram's Garden) and Pennypack Park in Northeast Philadelphia. They often range into nearby neighborhoods. The Southwest Philly turkeys occasionally show up along Baltimore Avenue.

KIDS: Spotting turkeys is a lot of fun with kids. These are large, easy-to-spot animals that even small children will recognize.

42

Touch Me Please
Squeeze Jewelweed Seed Pods

I HAVE LEARNED THE HAZARDS of taking a family hike past a patch of jewelweed at the end of the summer. Once, we were exploring the trails around the Pennypack Environmental Center. I thought two adults would be sufficient to wrangle two six-year-olds, but a large patch of jewelweed along the creek proved us wrong. The flowers are nice to look at, and indeed they are closely related to the tropical impatiens that are popular yard flowers. The jewelweed flowers mature into half-inch seed pods looking like little green footballs, just like those of the often-planted impatiens. Touch those "touch-me-not" pods and they explode, scattering the seeds so that they can sprout the following spring.

The challenge is that this is a bit addictive, and kids (and adults, as I have learned) can easily get hooked on touching every mature seed pod they can find to make them explode. Maybe it isn't a challenge but the best kind of diversion. Any excuse to make botany fun and discuss seed dispersal adaptations is a win for a nature walk, although you might run out of time for anything else.

Keep an eye out for jewelweed as you go on nature walks through the spring and summer. They tend to grow in dense patches in wet soil near waterways or wetlands. What starts as a carpet of little plants with gently serrated leaves sprouting out of the mud surges into a five-foot-tall thicket dotted with orange or yellow flowers (depending on the species). Take note of where you're seeing them and then come back in September. You barely need to brush ripe seed pods to get them to explode, and once you get one to pop, your walking companions will get the idea and dive in.

Jewelweed grows in moist areas near the Pennypack Environmental Center, on the way to the creek from the historic Verree House as well as other spots along the banks of the creek.

WHERE: The Pennypack Environmental Center is located off Verree Road in Northeast Philadelphia.

ACCESS: The center can be reached by car or by the 67 SEPTA bus. The trails are natural surface.

WHEN: Late summer into early fall

FOR MORE INFORMATION: Check out the center's Facebook page (https://www.facebook.com/PennypackEnvironmentalCenter/) for hours and information about walks and other programming.

EQUIPMENT: Wear shoes suitable for uneven woodland trails as well as a little mud.

GUIDED VIEWING: The Pennypack Environmental Center offers a full schedule of nature walks and other programming.

OTHER LOCATIONS: Jewelweed is a common plant in our area, so keep an eye out for a patch whenever you are near water.

KIDS: This is incredibly fun for kids of all ages and a great introduction to seed dispersal strategies. So many of these strategies are also fun for kids to talk about—for example, wild cherries that birds eat and then poop out far away, acorns buried by jays and squirrels, or the samaras of maple trees that spin and drift through the air, landing far from the parent tree.

43

Rising through the Cracks
Study Sidewalk Crack Plants

I WAS WALKING ALONG with a Philadelphia Botanical Club outing, trying to keep up with the plants being named—very few of which sounded familiar to me—when I caught one I knew: epazote. I interrupted the leader to confirm, "the herb from Mexican cuisine?" Indeed, that was the very same plant. Plucked from the sidewalks on my block, it tastes great in a pot of beans.[1]

Thus began my love affair with sidewalk-crack plants. Few have proven as tasty as the epazote, but even when the jungle is only concrete, plants are growing that we can learn about. They can also play a role in our block-level ecosystems. For example, in early fall, at least a couple of species of aster bloom from the edges of sidewalks, serving as feeding stations for the remaining pollinators. Carpenter bees packing up a nest to survive through the winter welcome the pollen and nectar. Buckeye and monarch butterflies fuel up before migrating south.

You might view sidewalk-crack plants as a nuisance to be weeded. Before you rip them out, take a minute to identify the weeds. Gardeners will recognize most of them—for example, purslane, with its fleshy leaves and flat growth habit, and, of course, dandelion, with

---

1. Only eat a plant if you are absolutely certain you know what it is. Some can make you sick, and a few can kill you.

its rosette of leaves with their toothy margins. You might also find escaped ornamental annuals, such as larkspurs or petunias.

Don't be shy about getting your face close to the pavement. Many familiar plants, such as plantain species or Japanese mazus, grow in miniature when they get stepped on a few times per day. They reward the close observer with itty-bitty, but beautiful, flowers. Brick paths can be particularly productive, with their abundance of interbrick spaces. Be sure to check damp, shaded spots for primitive plants like mosses and liverworts.

WHERE: Your block

EQUIPMENT: A magnifying glass will come in handy. There are lots of general plant guidebooks that will also help, but *Wild Urban Plants of the Northeast: A Guidebook* by Peter Del Tredici is particularly well suited to sidewalk botanizing. iNaturalist or other plant identification apps can help as well.

GUIDED VIEWING: Most nature centers and arboretums offer plant identification walks. Even if these are in greener settings than a sidewalk, the same skills and techniques apply. If you get hooked on observing plants, consider joining the Philadelphia Botanical Club and coming along on their walks as well.

KIDS: This is well suited for children. Even if they're not old enough to work through plant guidebooks or have an iNaturalist account, they can get down close to the ground with a magnifying glass and enjoy the tiny world revealed right outside their door.

44

Low Light Hightailing
Watch Deer at Dusk

I SPOTTED THE DEER UP THE HILL in the cemetery, four or five of them eating with their heads down and one with his head up, looking right back at me. For that second, I got to admire him, muscles bulging under his tawny coat, his head crowned by antlers. Then, he snorted, and the others picked their heads up. I took another step forward, and they bounded off into the woods.

Philadelphia park and suburban landscapes offer endless edge habitat (where fields meet woods) that white-tailed deer prefer, and almost nothing hunts them: There are no mountain lions or wolves. Virtually no humans shoot at them outside of a few resourceful bowhunters and sharpshooters hired by parks to control local deer populations. The result is that urban and suburban parks are possibly the easiest places ever to observe deer.

In the Philadelphia area, white-tailed deer are often discussed as overpopulated pests, devouring tree saplings and stripping native plants from our forests. That is true. Nonetheless, they are crowd pleasers, combining grace and power like no other creature in the urban landscape.

Deer are most active at dawn and dusk (making them neither diurnal nor nocturnal but rather "crepuscular"). To find them, head out after dinner and walk through fields near those edges they favor. If you're walking with a group (particularly if that group has some kids who have trouble keeping quiet), make sure that whoever is in front is watching as far out ahead as possible. Deer have evolved with thirteen thousand years or so of human hunting, so

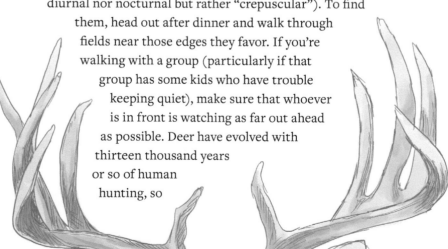

even in parks with tons of people, they do their best to avoid us. At some point, the deer will decide it's best to take off, but, of course, half the fun is watching them lift their white tails like flags and bound fifteen feet like it's nothing at all.

Even when you're not seeing deer in the flesh, learn to observe their tracks and other signs. Keep an eye on muddy sections of the trail for their hoofprints and look for places where vegetation is matted down and scattered with deer droppings, indications that deer have been taking a break. You can also find tree saplings that have been ripped up by bucks rubbing their antlers.

WHERE: The Mount Moriah Cemetery straddles Cobbs Creek at the border of Southwest Philadelphia and Delaware County. As an old, bucolic cemetery, it is a lovely place for a walk for any reason, but keep an eye on where the open cemetery meets the woods along the creek.

ACCESS: The cemetery is open from dawn to dusk. There is no parking lot, but there is street parking nearby. The 13 trolley passes by the cemetery. Some paths are paved, while others are brick and grass.

WHEN: Autumn is a great time to spot deer, particularly with the bucks in fighting form with full racks, although you can observe deer throughout the year.

FOR MORE INFORMATION: Visit the Friends of Mount Moriah Cemetery website (https://friendsofmountmoriahcemetery.org/) for more information about the cemetery.

EQUIPMENT: Deer are easy to observe with the naked eye, and comfortable walking shoes will suffice. Binoculars can help you observe them from farther away.

GUIDED VIEWING: Check the Friends of Mount Moriah Cemetery online calendar for occasional nature walks. Nature walks at other parks and nature centers frequently include observations of deer or their signs.

OTHER LOCATIONS: Deer are easy to observe along field edges throughout our region.

KIDS: Watching deer is a lot of fun for kids of any age.

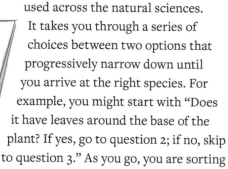

45

Identity Check
Key Out Wildflowers

EVERY YEAR, STARTING IN AUGUST and lasting into the fall, I enjoy the visual bounty of the yellow wildflowers that blaze from open fields and even light up patches in shady forests. The problem is I can't tell one species of goldenrod from another. And every year, I say I'm going to learn goldenrod next year, but this is finally the year.

Although you can identify most plants you find with iNaturalist or another phone-based app, the human brain is even faster and more accurate when trained on real-life examples. Before you know it, you'll be taking a quick look at the distinguishing features (Leaves fuzzy or smooth? Flowers clustered at the top or spread up and down the stem?) and identifying plants faster than you can whip out your phone.

The dichotomous key is a written identification tool used across the natural sciences. It takes you through a series of choices between two options that progressively narrow down until you arrive at the right species. For example, you might start with "Does it have leaves around the base of the plant? If yes, go to question 2; if no, skip to question 3." As you go, you are sorting between smaller and smaller groups of options until you land on the only choice left.

Although you can do this in the field, it is more comfortable to examine the plants in question at a well-lit table or desk with all the tools you'll need at hand (just be sure to take photos of any parts of the plants you don't take home with you, in case a detail about the leaves at the base, for example, proves to be important). A magnifying glass and ruler will help as you study smaller features like bracts, the little scales that line the base of each flower head. And, of course, you'll need your key, whether you're working with an online, interactive key or an old-fashioned printed version.

The hardest part is probably the terminology. You might need basic plant diagrams for parts you might not have heard of (pappus? capitulescence?) and likely a glossary for the jargon. Botanists sometimes use familiar terms in unfamiliar ways, such as "pubescent" instead of "fuzzy."

WHERE: Pick wildflowers from vacant lots, the sidewalk, weedy patches in your garden, or other places where it is allowed (when in doubt, ask) and take them home to examine more closely.

WHEN: The end of summer and early fall bring a bounty of wildflowers.

FOR MORE INFORMATION: A comprehensive plant guide like *The Plants of Pennsylvania* is a good place to start for a key, but more limited guides like *Newcomb's Wildflower Guide* will still cover most of what you are likely to find. Online, the Native Plant Trust's website (https://gobotany.nativeplanttrust.org/) has an easy-to-use key. It was built for New England species but covers most of what you'll find here.

EQUIPMENT: You'll need a key, either printed in a plant guidebook or online, as well as a magnifying glass or loupe to examine the plants closely.

GUIDED VIEWING: You can tackle all of this on your own, but it helps to have a class to work with. You'll soon get the hang of it, and, more importantly, you'll be able to appreciate the diversity revealed once you can quickly identify plants. Local arboretums and nature centers offer plant identification workshops, with some of them, such as Morris Arboretum in Chestnut Hill, offering identification classes focused on fall wildflowers.

KIDS: Working through a key might be challenging for younger children, but older kids with a methodical disposition can enjoy keying out plants.

46

Who Goes There?
Stake Out Your Yard for Nocturnal Mammals

It was a little after 10 p.m. when I
stepped out of our back door to check for moths.
This was during the 2019 City Nature Challenge, and
I was hoping to rack up a few more species before I got ready for bed.
Out of the darkness at the edge of our backyard (at 20 × 8 ft, calling
it a "yard" is generous), a cat-sized, pale-furred creature ambled into
view, seemingly oblivious to me. Only a few feet away, the opossum
looked up, considered me for a moment, and then turned around
and left.

Mid-sized or large diurnal (active during the day) mammals
generally don't do well in cities. They end up trying to cross roads
when traffic is heaviest, and humans tend to notice them more,
which generally doesn't go well for
the animal. The urban survivors
work around our schedules.
If you'd like to observe
the raccoons, opossums,
foxes, and possibly even
the coyotes in your
neighborhood, you have
to do it at night.

If you have a yard,
even a tiny urban yard,
then you can hang out
after dark and keep
as still and quiet as
possible. You are on a
stakeout, so bring the
beverage of your choice,

set up a comfortable lawn chair, and let your eyes adjust to the dark. Bring a flashlight, but keep it turned off as much as possible to preserve your night vision.

If you don't have the time and patience for a proper stakeout, consider investing $50 or so in a game camera. Battery-powered, infrared-triggered cameras are used for research into the habits of all sorts of animals. The same basic technique used by snow leopard researchers in the Himalayas can work in your backyard. You can review the images captured the next morning and see what showed up while you slept. Do be careful about where you point the camera so as not to capture images of your neighbors outside your property, something that ranges from inconsiderate to illegal, depending on your local laws.

WHERE: Your yard or garden

WHEN: You can do this at any time of the year.

EQUIPMENT: For live observation, it's good to have a comfortable place to sit and a flashlight. You can buy battery-powered game cameras online or at outdoor sporting goods shops.

GUIDED VIEWING: Plenty of nature centers and parks offer night hikes. This can be a great way to get an expert's training on observing wildlife at night.

OTHER LOCATIONS: If you don't have a yard, check out a night hike in a local park or check with neighbors or local community gardens to see whether you can access their properties after dark.

KIDS: On the one hand, this is an easy activity suitable for any child old enough to sit still and be quiet. On the other, it might require staying up after bedtime. Picking a night when the sun sets earlier (fall through spring) might make the most sense for younger children (and don't forget the hot chocolate).

47

Tall, Dark, and Ancient
Hike an Old-Growth Forest

IN EARLY SPRING, I found myself staring high into the trees in Carpenter's Woods in the Mount Airy neighborhood of Philadelphia, trying to get a good look at the warblers making their way through the canopy. This was not easy because the trees of Carpenter's Woods are about as tall as you'll find in the area, columns of tree trunks climbing high to a distant canopy.

Pennsylvania (Penn's Woods) is full of forests, but they are mostly young as forests go. The state was thoroughly logged well into the 1800s. Through the 1900s and into the current century, logged hillsides, old crop fields, and pastures have been abandoned to the trees. Over time, in some cases assisted by thinning and fire, these forests can mature into landscapes of larger trees, relatively spaced out. There is no universal definition of an old-growth forest, but woods that have escaped logging for a couple of centuries and are composed of trees that have grown about as tall and thick as possible play important roles in the broader landscape. For example, they store an enormous amount of carbon, and they serve as habitat for species that need large hollow trees. Carpenter's Woods has been designated an old-growth forest by the Old-Growth Forest Network.[1]

---

1. Old-Growth Forest Network, "Carpenter's Woods - Wissahickon Valley Park," accessed October 29, 2020, https://www.oldgrowthforest.net/pa-carpenters-woods-wissahickon-valley-park.

WHERE: Carpenter's Woods includes several trailheads, but it's easy to start where Wayne Avenue dead-ends into West Sedgwick.

ACCESS: The park is open from dawn till dusk. The trails are natural surface. Carpenter's Woods is easily reached on the 53 bus.

WHEN: Year-round

FOR MORE INFORMATION: Visit the Friends of Carpenter's Woods website (https://www.focw.org) for more information, including on service events and guided walks. You can also view a map of significant trees there (https://www.focw.org/wp-content/uploads/2018/07/focw-tree-map.pdf).

EQUIPMENT: Shoes suitable for forest trails are sufficient.

GUIDED VIEWING: Spring is an especially good time of year for guided walks, particularly bird-themed, but you can also find walks focusing on other life, such as plants or reptiles and amphibians.

OTHER LOCATIONS: Hart's Woods Preserve in Bucks County is also part of the Old-Growth Forest Network, and you can find old stands in other parks and preserves throughout the region.

KIDS: Old trees might seem big to adults, but they are even more enormous and grand the smaller we are. The trails through Carpenter's Woods make for easy hikes for kids. Warning: Off-leash dogs can be a problem at Carpenter's Woods.

At Carpenter's Woods, you can find stands of oaks (red, white, black), beech, and tulip trees that are more than two hundred years old. These enormous trees host screech and barred owls as well as flying squirrels. The forest stands out to the songbirds migrating along the Atlantic Flyway, making it a popular place for birders to spot warblers, vireos, thrushes, and other species during spring and fall migration.

Seeing big trees and wildlife is reason enough to visit, but a walk through an old-growth forest like Carpenter's Woods can reset your baseline of what a forest can be. Younger woods can have a scrubby quality, with small trees packed together, draped with vines and difficult to walk through. More mature woods often have an open feel, with much of the greenery well above your heads and the farther-spaced trees offering longer lines of sight.

48
No Lungs? No Problem
Find Red-Backed Salamanders (and Lots of Other Cool Critters) under Stuff

RED-BACKED SALAMANDERS saved the nature walk for me. I had taken a group of families out on a trail in the Wissahickon Valley in Philadelphia, and after an hour and a half, we hadn't turned up very much. As the group dragged out along the trail, conversation shifted to the kids' soccer leagues and plans for after the walk. Turning over a log to reveal small, almost cartoonishly cute red-backed salamanders turned the mood around in a flash. Everyone leaned in to take a closer look, and the kids started looking around for more logs to roll.

These woodland salamanders, fully grown at four inches, live in the leaf litter of forests throughout the region. As critters that cumulatively eat tons of invertebrates and are in turn gobbled up by a long list of predators, they play a key role in forest ecology. When you look for them, you'll also find an assortment of other small critters (beetles, ants, worms, and centipedes, to name a few) that share their forest floor habitat and play critical roles behind the scenes in the forest.

Finding red-backed salamanders is as easy as heading into the woods and looking under rocks and logs. Lift or roll any cover object very carefully and let it down gently when you're done, making sure to leave it exactly how you found it. These delicate creatures are vulnerable to heat, desiccation, and chemicals on our skin, so handle them as little as possible and use a clean jar if you'd like to pass them around or take pictures. Release the salamanders *after* you replace the log or rock. You'll avoid squashing them, and they'll find their way back underneath.

Red-backed salamanders prefer cool weather, so you won't find them near the surface in the middle of summer. Search for them from when temperatures drop in the fall until they start to rise again in May.

WHERE: The Wissahickon Valley in Northwest Philadelphia covers eighteen hundred acres, most of it forested, and most of it suitable for salamanders.

ACCESS: Wissahickon Valley's extensive trail network has numerous access points. The trails where you'll find salamanders are generally natural surface.

WHEN: Red-backed salamanders avoid freezing weather and the heat of the summer by retreating underground. It is easiest to find them in the fall and the spring, but you can also find them on warmer winter days.

FOR MORE INFORMATION: Check out the Friends of the Wissahickon website (https://fow.org) for information on the park as well as a schedule of nature walks and other events.

EQUIPMENT: Bring a clean jar to hold them so you can take a closer look. A magnifying glass will reveal the full detail of their rich, iridescent patterns.

OTHER LOCATIONS: Most wooded parks and even some shaded yards host populations of red-backed salamanders. Next time you're on a walk in the woods, take a moment to look under a log or two.

KIDS: Looking under rocks and logs and finding all sorts of worms, centipedes, beetles, and other critters is a perfect children's nature activity. Supervise younger children to be sure that they handle animals gently and don't love them to death.

49

Headstone Garden
Search for Cemetery Lichens

On a walk at Laurel Hill Cemetery, we searched for lichens growing on headstones. Lichens seem to jump out at me, in the sense that I'll often be looking at a brick wall, a tree trunk, a wood bench—almost any outdoor object—and suddenly my brain realizes that there is indeed something growing there. Suddenly, the apparently dead surface is alive. At the cemetery, the headstones were no longer simply records of the people buried beneath the green grass; they were themselves gardens, alive with the leafy gray circles of a common green shield and the greenish-yellow patches of candleflame lichen.

Lichens manage to grow on dry, inhospitable places where plants, even mosses, can't get a foothold. That might mean the dry surfaces of tree bark or rocks. Cities are largely built from rock, natural and artificial (like brick), meaning that lichens are all around us.

Every lichen is a "composite organism." A fungus provides the structure, and an alga grows within it and conducts photosynthesis, essentially feeding the fungus in a mutually beneficial relationship. Lichens can be roughly grouped into three categories based on how they grow. Foliose lichens have a flat, leaflike structure growing from anchor points and look a bit like leaves. Fruticose lichens project out much more from the surface, sometimes looking bushy or hairy. Crustose lichens grow just like their name sounds, as crusts stuck to the surface.[1]

---

1. U.S. Forest Service, "Lichen Biology," accessed October 29, 2020, https://www
.fs.fed.us/wildflowers/beauty/lichens/biology.shtml.

Historic cemeteries are full of old stone surfaces and the trunks of stately trees where lichens have had plenty of time to grow and are easy to observe. Polished marble tends not to give lichen spores anywhere to gain a foothold, but older, weathered stone can become positively cloaked in lichens. Although you can see plenty of lichens with the naked eye, a magnifying glass can help you tell when a patch of off-colored stone is actually a gray crust lichen with a low profile. Magnification can also reveal additional detail, such as spots on the lichen that are actually cuplike reproductive structures, ready to release spores.

WHERE: Laurel Hill Cemetery is located just off Kelly Drive in Philadelphia and is easy to reach by car, by SEPTA, or by foot off the Schuylkill River Trail. Check its website (https://thelaurelhillcemetery.org/) for details.

ACCESS: Laurel Hill Cemetery is open year-round, but the hours change depending on the season, so check the website to confirm when it is open. Many of the paths through the cemetery are paved.

WHEN: Lichens are observable year-round.

FOR MORE INFORMATION: Local botanical and mycology clubs lead occasional lichen walks. Laurel Hill Cemetery has a full calendar of cultural, historical, and nature events. Check its website (https://thelaurelhillcemetery.org/) for details.

EQUIPMENT: Wear whatever you would for a walk in a cemetery and bring a magnifying glass.

OTHER LOCATIONS: Old cemeteries everywhere are lovely places to spend a quiet morning or afternoon studying lichens. And, of course, lichens grow practically everywhere there is bark, stone, brick, or concrete, so you can get started on your stoop or in your garden.

KIDS: This is an easy activity for children of all ages. You can make it a game to see which headstone has the most species growing on it. If their attention to lichens wanes, Laurel Hill, like all cemeteries, is still a great place to wander and explore.

50

Mussel Building
Visit the Mussel Hatchery

FRESHWATER MUSSELS MIGHT NOT LOOK like much (generally, rough brown lumps half-buried in the mud and sand at the bottom of the river), but they are critical to keeping our rivers clean, each one filtering ten gallons of water per day. Multiply that impact by the thousands packed into "beds" along the river bottom, and you've got an important water purification system. Unfortunately, decades of pollution along with centuries of dams on our waterways have devastated many of our mussel beds.

Baby mussels, which cannot swim and would otherwise be swept away with the current, depend on fish to hitch a ride upstream (mussels shoot their larvae into a fish's face so that a few latch onto the gills), where they drop off and settle into the mud for decades of filter feeding. If the fish can't make it around a dam, neither can the

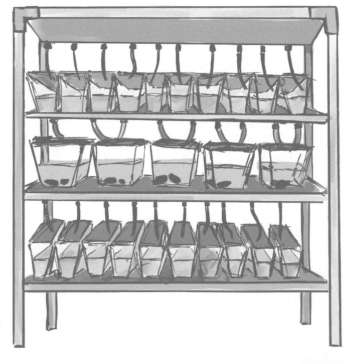

mussels. Luckily, local organizations, led by the Partnership for the Delaware Estuary, are working to hatch mussels and release them where the fish can't reach.

Keep an eye out for mussel shells the next time you're walking along the shore of one of our creeks or rivers. Different species of mussels have different shell shapes, but generally, they'll be longer than they are wide, not as evenly rounded as the Asian clam shells you will likely also find, and larger than the saltwater mussels you might eat. A pile of shells indicates where a predator, such as an otter, has been feeding on mussels dragged up from the bottom.

Although you can find their remains on the shore, it is difficult to observe mussels in action. All the exciting stuff usually happens under many feet of opaque water.

Luckily, you can watch the action live at the Fairmount Water Works Mussel Hatchery, which combines an active mussel laboratory with a museum exhibit. There, racks of fish tanks host mussels at various stages of development. Scientists coax gravid mussels to release their larvae so that they can be raised and ultimately released back into our waterways. Visitors can touch mussel shells and learn about their life cycle and importance to the Delaware watershed. Next time you find a mussel shell, you'll know more about the life it lived.

WHERE: The Fairmount Water Works is located between Boathouse Row and the Philadelphia Museum of Art, off Kelly Drive.

ACCESS: The Fairmount Water Works is free to the general public and is open Tuesday through Saturday, 10:00 A.M. to 5:00 P.M., and Sunday, 1:00 to 5:00 P.M. It is closed Monday. It is wheelchair-accessible and easily reached from the 38 bus stop behind the Philadelphia Museum of Art.

FOR MORE INFORMATION: Visit its website (https://fairmountwater works.org) and the hatchery's companion website (https://mighty mussel.com).

KIDS: This exhibit is well suited for children.

51

Rats with Wings and Other Common Birds
Start Birding Anytime

THE ACTION WAS FIERCE. A small group of house sparrows was brawling, chirping up a racket as a female attacked a male, darting in to bite him as he fled. She got a grip on the feathers on his head and yanked him into the air. I stood outside the old office building on the sidewalk, joined by a woman who, after watching for a moment, turned to me and exclaimed, "They're mad about something!"

Familiarity breeds contempt for our most abundant urban birds, none of them native: house sparrows, European starlings, and pigeons (aka rock doves or "rats with wings"). Rare warblers they ain't, but they are still worthy of our observation, and they offer the beginning birder easy access to develop skills that will come in handy with any feathered friends.

Even before you pick up your first binoculars, you can start learning from the birds on your block. Start a daily journal: When do the male house sparrows claim nest holes and start singing outside them? When do the fledgling starlings appear, hiding in

the flower beds like grumpy little dinosaurs? And when you get your hands on binoculars, you can practice focusing and getting your target into view (harder than it looks) with the birds flying all around you.

Studying bird behavior and ecology on your block will serve you as you venture farther afield, and familiarity with common birds will help you distinguish others by comparison. You'll notice that the birds that landed in that crabapple tree with a high-pitched chorus of uniform calls don't sound like starlings. They're cedar waxwings. The sparrow-sized bird that kind of sounds like it's crying and flies in a bouncy style is a goldfinch. That bird with the longer tail flying at the edge of the pigeon flock—indeed, *pursuing* the pigeon flock—is actually a Cooper's hawk.

WHERE: Any urban area will have at least one and probably all three of these easily observable, so your block is a great place to start. Urban parks like Washington Square, where people drop crumbs either by accident as they eat lunch or on purpose to feed birds, are also easy places to sit back on a park bench and observe.

ACCESS: You can observe these birds from any sidewalk or porch in our area.

WHEN: You can observe these birds year-round.

EQUIPMENT: Binoculars will help, but they're not necessary. Take notes in a notebook or a notes app on your phone.

GUIDED VIEWING: You can learn birding basics with such programs as BirdPhilly's guided walks (learn more at https://birdphilly.org) and Birding Backpacks that you can check out of your local library.

KIDS: This is a great way for kids to start birding. They don't need any equipment, and they don't even need to leave their block.

52

Autumn Glow
Take a Walk in a Field of Wildflowers

A SCENIC HIKE ISN'T JUST ABOUT WHERE but when. One of the region's most beautiful hikes is through Houston Meadow, part of the Wissahickon Valley Park in Philadelphia, as summer transitions to fall. Goldenrods and bonesets paint the hillside in white and yellow, all framed by the wooded valley in the background. Look closer and you'll see white heath asters arching down toward the trail, and magenta New England asters will pop into view.

The first wildflowers of spring rightly demand our attention after the colorless winter. Then, through the summer, other blooms take their turns in our gardens and beyond. By the end of the season, you might be excused for barely glancing at the fall wildflowers. Change your mind and get excited with a trip to Houston Meadow in the Andorra neighborhood of Philadelphia. This meadow, restored around 2013 after decades of having its edges nibbled away by encroaching forest, offers what is locally a rare habitat type.

Of course, we are not the flowers' target audience. This "fall nectar flow" makes the meadow a wonderful place to observe bees and butterflies pigging out on the fall bounty. Keep an eye out for other calm and charismatic insects, such as the black-and-yellow wasp-mimic black locust borer beetle and the Ailanthus web moth,

with its bright orange, black, and white wings tucked in like a beetle. Bring a magnifying glass and inspect the spaces in between and behind flowers for cryptic predators, such as crab spiders and assassin bugs.

WHERE: The Houston Meadow is in the Andorra neighborhood of Northwest Philadelphia.

ACCESS: The trails of the Wissahickon Valley, including those through Houston Meadow, are open from dawn to dusk, and they are natural surface. You can access the meadow from the network of trails in the Wissahickon Valley as well from trailheads at the Houston Playground or the Courtesy Stable on East Cathedral Road. The 62 bus runs about a block from both trailheads.

WHEN: The wildflower bloom peaks from late summer into early autumn.

FOR MORE INFORMATION: Check out the Friends of the Wissahickon website (https://fow.org) and social media for more information about Houston Meadow as well as upcoming walks and volunteer events.

EQUIPMENT: Binoculars will come in handy to view butterflies, but they aren't essential. Hiking shoes or sneakers with good tread will suffice.

GUIDED VIEWING: The Friends of the Wissahickon, the Wissahickon Environmental Center, and multiple other groups offer guided walks through Houston Meadow, but the Friends of the Wissahickon calendar is a good place to start to learn more about upcoming walks.

OTHER LOCATIONS: You can check out similar scenes anywhere you find a meadow. Formal meadows at parks are great, but don't forget to check out power line cuts, vacant lots, railroad rights-of-way, and the edges of mowed fields and fence lines. I have found goldenrod growing in alleyways, and several asters are common sidewalk-crack plants. These weedy fall asters draw such pollinators as buckeye butterflies and carpenter bees, those hulking nectar supertankers, to the most urban corners of the city.

KIDS: What child doesn't love chasing butterflies around? Bees are easy to get close to when their faces are buried in flowers.

Take Action

I HOPE THAT READING THIS BOOK has you itching to get outside and start exploring. As you become more comfortable and experienced exploring your neighborhood, though, you might wonder what you can do to better welcome nature.

Some challenges to welcoming nature are inherent to the urban landscape and particularly difficult to get around. It will take some big, creative work to build a city out of greener stuff than asphalt and concrete, and roads will continue to impose barriers to animals that travel on the ground.

We can still do a lot, however, to make our neighborhoods friendlier to our wild neighbors.

For birds in particular, we can make our buildings more friendly by making glass visible to them, particularly when the glass reflects vegetation. A bird that has spent its entire life in a forest flies at full speed for the tree or bushes it sees, not understanding that some are reflections on a rock-hard surface. Hundreds of millions of birds die in North America every year by colliding with glass. While large glass-surfaced buildings draw attention for killing lots of birds, even more die on the windows of houses and other small buildings. They die in ones and twos, but they add up. Luckily, there are lots of ways to make your windows more visible to birds, ranging from buying glass with visible patterns on it to simply painting vertical lines with washable paint during spring and fall migration.[1] Check out

---

1. American Bird Conservancy, "Glass Collisions," accessed October 29, 2020, https://abcbirds.org/program/glass-collisions/.

the American Bird Conservancy's website (https://abcbirds.org) for details on how you can make your windows safer for birds.

Keep cats inside. They kill billions of birds and other small animals each year, and they do it completely unnecessarily. Cats stalk, grab, and bite small moving objects for fun, as any cat owner who has watched their pet play with a toy mouse on a string knows. When that small moving object is alive, it dies. This spring, I found several dead starling fledglings on my block, some with the impressions of cat teeth still visible. Each was caught by a cat that dropped the bird when it wasn't entertaining anymore. And cats don't stop with birds—they kill snakes, frogs, and native small mammals, such as shrews and rabbits.[2] You can immediately make your neighborhood more hospitable to wildlife by keeping your cat inside.

If you want it to get some fresh air, take it out on a leash where you can supervise it or build it an enclosed "catio" where it can enjoy the outdoors while keeping wildlife safe. Of course, this is safer for the cat too. I routinely see cats dead on the road, and outdoor cats are also vulnerable to dogs, coyotes, poisoning, and diseases they can catch from other cats.

Also, resist the urge to feed stray cats. Cats, like every other animal in the world, are attracted to food. By offering them food, you keep them on your block, where they will keep on killing other creatures. Cat food left outside also feeds rats (which cats generally don't kill) as well as larger mammals, such as raccoons, foxes, and skunks, bringing them into conflict with your neighbors and making it easier for them to spread diseases, such as rabies.

Planting more plants, particularly native plants, will be a big help. Plenty of local organizations can help you incorporate more native plants into your garden. Several nature centers, such as the Schuylkill Center for Environmental Education, feature

---

2. S. Loss, T. Will, and P. Marra, "The Impact of Free-Ranging Domestic Cats on Wildlife of the United States," *Nature Communications* 4 (2013): 1396, doi:10.1038/ncomms2380.

demonstration gardens with native species, as does the Lower
Merion Conservancy's headquarters in Rolling Hill Park in Gladwyn.
The Natural Lands' Stoneleigh Natural Garden in Villanova shows
how native plants can be incorporated on a large scale into formal
gardening, and A Child's Inspiration: Wildlife Discovery Garden
in Philadelphia's Fishtown neighborhood shows how the same
can be done on the scale of a small urban lot. Green stormwater
infrastructure plantings (meant to soak up rainwater and avoid
sewage overflows after heavy rain) have made extensive use of native
plants—for example, the Tookany/Tacony-Frankford Watershed
Partnership's plantings at Ethel M. Jordan Memorial Park in Elkins
Park. The Philadelphia Water Department's plantings featuring
native species have meant that native plant landscaping can be
viewed throughout the city of Philadelphia.

You can purchase native plants at specialized nurseries, such
as Redbud in Media and Good Host Plants in Philadelphia. You can
also often buy native plants at sales at local nature centers, public
gardens, and arboretums.

Native plants' fruit and flowers are important, of course, but
perhaps more important is that our native bugs have evolved to eat
them. The more bugs we have, the more food we provide for the
critters that eat bugs, such as frogs, bats, and birds. The next time
you are watching insectivorous birds, such as warblers in a park, note
how much more time those birds spend in the native oaks, cherries,
or willows compared to the exotic gingkos or princess trees. The
more we plant native vegetation, the more we create habitats for
bugs and everything else up the food chain.

That leads me to a recommendation that might be harder to
sell: Embrace bugs. Nature writers like me too often justify bugs
as instrumental to some other end: Pollinators help us grow food,
dragonflies eat mosquitoes, and moths are food for birds. Let's
recognize that our invertebrates are beautiful in their own right and
that we should do our best to welcome them for that reason alone.

I am not arguing that anyone should put up with mosquitoes
biting them or pantry moths in their cereal. But outside of a few

species that directly affect us, the vast majority of our arthropods pose no threat whatsoever. I'm talking about thousands of species that carry on their lives outside and simply want to stay out of our way.

You can welcome your local invertebrates by adding some complexity to your garden. Keeping fallen leaves on the ground rather than raking them up and leaving dead wood to decompose are two easy steps to offer more housing and food. Many bee species will nest in bare patches of soil or sand. Others will use hollow plant stems, and bee apartment blocks, which consist of bundles of hollow stems or wood blocks with holes drilled through, can provide nesting spots for these species.

If nothing else, you can reduce your use of chemical insecticides. Whatever you're spraying for, that spray will kill other bugs too. You can also retire the bug zapper. The ultraviolet light they use draws in relatively few mosquitoes.[3] The little cracks you hear are mostly the electrocutions of moths and other critters that pose no threat to us. Your local agricultural extension office offers Integrated Pest Management (IPM) resources. Start there if you've got a pest problem. And if something lands on your arm in your garden and it's not a mosquito, you can simply shake it off. Better yet, reach for your magnifying glass.

Beyond your block, consider supporting the organizations that maintain our green spaces. I haven't met a friends group that isn't looking for donations or volunteers to clean up trash, fight invasive plants, plant trees, or otherwise get their hands dirty. If you live near a well-resourced green space, please consider supporting one in a lower-resource neighborhood. In Philadelphia, an inequitable result of reduced government parks spending is that wealthier neighbors step in to support their neighborhood parks to a degree that people

---

3. Timothy B. Frick and Douglas W. Tallamy, "Density and Diversity of Nontarget Insects Killed by Suburban Electric Insect Traps," *Entomological News* 107, no. 2 (March/April 1996): 77–82.

in lower-resourced neighborhoods cannot, resulting in cleaner, better-maintained green spaces in wealthier neighborhoods.

Finally, teach your neighbors about the nature around them. If you're standing on the corner with your binoculars, watching the local red-tailed hawk eat a rat, let the kids on your block take a turn. If you see Philadelphia fleabanes blooming in the lot on the corner, let the neighbors on your block email list or social media network know about it. We can all be students of nature wherever we are, and we can be teachers as well.

Conclusion

The conventional notion that nature is something out in the country that you have to travel to in order to enjoy assumes a certain amount of privilege. It assumes that you have the money and means to travel to wild spaces. It assumes that you are physically capable of traversing rugged terrain. It also assumes that you have nothing to fear from racism in predominantly white rural communities.

Of course, all these barriers to enjoying parks and other green spaces need to be tackled—we need to combat racism, make parks more accessible, and improve public transportation systems—but I hope that redefining our routine, everyday spaces as places where we can connect with and learn from nature opens the experience to more of us.

A theme of this book has been that exploring nature is for everyone and that more people can explore nature if we recognize that we can explore nature everywhere. Beyond that, I hope that recognizing the value of urban spaces as natural spaces leads us to value all our fellow urban naturalists as students, companions, and teachers.

Acknowledgments

I NEED TO START by thanking Aaron Javsicas at Temple University Press for his collaboration, guidance, and, most of all, patience. This is my first book, and he bore the brunt of my inexperience.

Sam Wittchen brought these activities to life with her illustrations and beyond that was a constant friend and cheerleader throughout the project. I hope we have many more opportunities to team up.

Philadelphia is blessed with a vibrant and collegial community of nature lovers, and this work would have been impossible without their fellowship, teaching, and encouragement over the years.

Specifically for this project, Scott McWilliams, Navin Sasikumar, Robin Irizarry, Tony Croasdale, and Ali Hurwitz read early drafts and provided indispensable fact checking, suggestions, and moral support.

On a City Nature Challenge nature walk at Fort Mifflin in 2019, I told Anne Bekker I was thinking of writing a book, and I thank her for acting like that was a totally reasonable aspiration and connecting me with Temple University Press.

I am not much of a photographer, and so I relied on naturalists who actually take good pictures. Thanks to Christian Hunold, Anne Bekker, Ryan Neuman, Navin Sasikumar, Brittany Stewart, John Jensen, Craig Johnson, Ken Frank, Judy Stepenaske, and David Fitzpatrick for their work.

Thanks to everyone who works to maintain our green spaces, educate Philadelphians about nature, and give nature writers like me something to write about. In particular, I'd like to thank the people who took time out of their busy days to answer my questions as I researched this book: Sandi Vincenti with A Child's Inspiration: Wildlife Discovery Garden; Kurt Cheng with the Partnership for the Delaware Estuary; George Armistead of the Delaware Valley Ornithological Club; Justin Dennis with the New Jersey Conservation Foundation; Allison Hartman with the Center for Aquatic Sciences at Adventure Aquarium; Emma Max of the Woodlands; Amy Chapkovich of the Lower Merion Conservancy; Kat Aboudara with Laurel Hill; Dennis Waters; Victoria Prizzia and Ellen Schultz with the Fairmount Water Works; Craig Johnson of Interpret Green; Wingyi Kung and David Stoughton with the John Heinz National Wildlife Refuge at Tinicum; Bill Reume; Carolyn Sutton of the Franklin Hawkaholics; Mike Weilbacher with the Schuylkill Center for Environmental Education; Tatyana Livshultz at the Academy of Natural Sciences of Drexel University; Cindy Skema of Morris Arboretum; Heather Zimmerman and Nancy Pasquier of Awbury Arboretum; Bill Woodroffe with the Churchville Nature Center; Kelly Herrenkohl of Natural Lands; Brian Green of Riverfront North; Julia Ehrhardt of Tyler Arboretum; and Julie Slavet with the Tookany/Tacony-Frankford Watershed Partnership.

Thanks to Alex Mulcahy for making *Grid* magazine my writing home for all these years.

I drew, implicitly if not explicitly, on the writing, research, and programming leadership of Ken Frank, Christian Hunold, Keith Russell, and David Hewitt.

Most of all, thank you to my family: Gigi Naglak for everything—for partnership, patience, edits, advice, picking up my slack at home, and putting up with all the mess of writing. And thank you to Magnolia and Gilda for being good sports, nature activity guinea pigs, and co-explorers on so many adventures. I look forward to a lifetime of many more adventures, everything from long hikes to just sitting by the window, watching chimney swifts.

Photo Captions
and Credits

Page 26: Bald Eagle, Credit: Anne Bekker
Page 28: House Centipede, Credit: Author
Page 30: Brown Rat, Credit: Ryan Neuman
Page 32: Cooper's Hawk, Credit: Christian Hunold
Page 34: Hugging a silver maple, Credit: Author
Page 36: Grey squirrel tracks in concrete, Credit: Author
Page 38: Cream violet collected by Thomas Porter in Manayunk in 1868,
  Credit: Philadelphia Herbarium (PH), The Academy of Natural Sciences
  of Drexel University, catalogue number PH00451227
Page 40: Snowy Owl, Credit: Navin Sasikumar
Page 42: Tulip Tree Bark, Credit: Author
Page 44: Raccoon, Credit: Author
Page 46: Ruddy Duck, Credit: Christian Hunold
Page 48: American Beaver, Credit: Christian Hunold
Page 50: Maple tree tapped to make syrup, Credit: Tony Croasdale
Page 54: Spring Beauties, Credit: John Jensen
Page 56: "Mom," the red-tailed hawk, Credit: Christian Hunold
Page 58: American Toad, Credit: Author
Page 60: Yellow Rumped Warbler, Credit: Christian Hunold
Page 62: Mid-Atlantic Leopard Frog, Credit: David Fitzpatrick
Page 64: Northern Brown Snake, Credit: Author
Page 66: Marsh Wren, Credit: Christian Hunold
Page 68: Philadelphia Fleabane, Credit: Author
Page 70: Water snake mating ball, Credit: Craig Johnson, Interpret Green
Page 72: Recording an observation for a bioblitz, Credit: Navin Sasikumar
Page 74: Peregrine falcons exchanging prey at the nest, Credit: Judith
  Stepenaskie
Page 76: Red-eared slider (right) and red-bellied turtle (left), Credit: Kenneth
  D. Frank

Page 78: Dog Vomit Slime Mold, Credit: Anne Bekker
Page 82: Common Nighthawk, Credit: Christian Hunold
Page 84: Fishing on the Delaware River, Credit: Riverfront North
Page 86: Paddling on the Delaware River, Credit: Center for Aquatic Sciences
Page 88: Common Eastern Firefly, Credit: Brittany Stewart
Page 90: Chicken of the Woods, Credit: Author
Page 92: Bridge spider capturing a moth in a web built under a lamp, Credit: Kenneth D. Frank
Page 94: Red Bat, Credit: Christian Hunold
Page 96: Green bottle fly killed by the fungus *Entomophthora muscae*, Credit: Author
Page 98: Red milkweed beetles on common milkweed, Credit: Author
Page 100: Eastern Tiger Swallowtail, Credit: Author
Page 102: Dogbane Tiger Moth and unidentified midges, Credit: Kenneth D. Frank
Page 104: Chimney swifts entering a chimney at Houston Elementary School, Credit: Anne Bekker
Page 106: Woodland Sunflower, Credit: Author
Page 110: Gray Squirrel, Credit: Christian Hunold
Page 112: Wild Turkey, Credit: Christian Hunold
Page 114: Jewelweed Seedpod, Credit: Author
Page 116: Slender Path Rush, Credit: Author
Page 118: White-Tailed Deer, Credit: Christian Hunold
Page 120: Blue-Stemmed Goldenrod, Credit: Author
Page 122: Virginia Opossum, Credit: Author
Page 124: Tree trunks in Carpenter's Woods, Credit: Author
Page 126: Red-Backed Salamander, Credit: Author
Page 128: An assortment of lichens, mostly *Physica millegrana*, *Candelaria concolor*, and *Flavoparmelia caperata*, Credit: Author
Page 130: Freshwater Mussel, likely *eastern elliptio*, Credit: Author
Page 132: European Starling, Credit: Anne Bekker
Page 134: Houston Meadow, Credit: Author

Bibliography

American Bird Conservancy. "Glass Collisions." https://abcbirds.org
/program/glass-collisions/.

Attenberg, Trevor. "Birding Blind: Open Your Ears to the Amazing World of
Bird Sounds." Audubon. https://www.audubon.org/news/birding-blind
-open-your-ears-amazing-world-bird-sounds.

Betancourt, Isa. "The Philadelphia Fountain Insect Survey." The Bug and
the Beetle. http://www.thebugandthebeetle.net/research.

Dimeler, Pamela. "Mom, 2017..." Facebook. March 21, 2019. https://www
.facebook.com/groups/FranklinHawkaholics/permalink
/10156472203392029.

Feinberg, Jeremy A., Catherine E. Newman, Gregory J. Watkins-Colwell,
Matthew D. Schlesinger, Brian Zarate, Brian R. Curry, H. Bradley
Shaffer, and Joanna Burger. "Cryptic Diversity in Metropolis:
Confirmation of a New Leopard Frog Species (Anura: Ranidae) from
New York City and Surrounding Atlantic Coast Regions." PLOS ONE 9,
no. 10 (October 2014). doi:10.1371/journal.pone.0108213.

Fort Mifflin. "The History of Fort Mifflin." http://www.fortmifflin.us/the
-history/.

Frick, Timothy B., and Douglas W. Tallamy. "Density and Diversity
of Nontarget Insects Killed by Suburban Electric Insect Traps."
Entomological News 107, no. 2 (March/April 1996): 77–82.

Hardisky, Tom. Beaver Management in Pennsylvania (2010–2019). Harrisburg,
PA: Pennsylvania Game Commission, 2011. https://www.pgc
.pa.gov/HuntTrap/TrappingandFurbearers/Documents/Beaver%20
Management%20in%20Pennsylvania%202010-2019.pdf.

Hewitt, David. "The White Pines of Cresheim Creek." Growing History, June
22, 2012. https://growinghistory.wordpress.com/2012/06/22/the-white
-pines-of-cresheim-creek/.

Loss, Scott R., Tom Will, and Peter P. Marra. "The Impact of Free-
Ranging Domestic Cats on Wildlife of the United States." *Nature
Communications* 4 (2013): 1396. doi:10.1038/ncomms2380.
Mid-Atlantic Herbaria Consortium. https://midatlanticherbaria.org/portal
/index.php.
Moore, Gerry. "An Overview of Scientific Names Honoring the City of
Philadelphia, Pennsylvania, with an Emphasis on Flowering Plants."
Bartonia, no. 69 (2016): 90–117. https://www.jstor.org/stable/44089931.
National Wild Turkey Federation. "Wild Turkey Population History and
Overview." https://www.nwtf.org/_resources/dyn/files/75706989
za3010574/_fn/Wild+Turkey+Population+History+and+Overview.pdf.
Old-Growth Forest Network. "Carpenter's Woods - Wissahickon Valley
Park." https://www.oldgrowthforest.net/pa-carpenters-woods-wissa
hickon-valley-park.
U.S. Forest Service. "Lichen Biology." https://www.fs.fed.us/wildflowers
/beauty/lichens/biology.shtml.
U.S. Geological Survey. "Geological Units in Philadelphia County,
Pennsylvania." https://mrdata.usgs.gov/geology/state/fips-unit
.php?code=f42101.
Walter, Robert C., and Dorothy J. Merritts. "Natural Streams and the
Legacy of Water-Powered Mills." *Science* 319, no. 5861 (January 18,
2008): 299–304. doi:10.1126/science.1151716.

Index

Bernard S. Brown is a nature writer for *Grid* magazine, cohost of the Urban Wildlife Podcast, and cofounder of the local nature hub PhillyNature.org.